WHAT PROFESSIONAL TRADERS REALLY USE

PRICE ACTION

Carlos B. Pascual
Engineer, Trader and Investor

What professional traders really use
Price action

ISBN: 978-3-00-085821-5
1st Edition, January 2026
Publisher: Dookke
Author: Carlos B. Pascual
With the support of

SI INVESTING

www.trading.si-investing.com

I would like to extend my heartfelt thanks, especially to Juan, Mike, and Søren, for the great conversations and your generosity in sharing ideas. Your inspiration has been invaluable in shaping the content of this book and the approaches I continue to explore. I look forward to continuing this journey together.

Thank you once again!

PROLOGUE

"What professional traders really use" is a step-by-step guide to reading and understanding charts and mastering price action and technical analysis like professional traders do. You'll find plenty of practical tools, professional secrets, and solid theory to enhance your daily trading.

You'll discover how to use candlesticks and chart patterns effectively and learn the logic behind price cycles and market movements. I will highlight and explain the key differences between mainstream techniques and the professional strategies.

While this book reveals powerful advanced techniques, it's structured in a way that's accessible and easy to follow, no matter where you are on your trading journey. It contains lots of real examples explained step by step and case studies to solidify your understanding.

You will also learn about common mistakes to avoid and proven recommendations to follow. Trading is a challenging mental competition both against others and against yourself.

I will also dive into the psychological side of trading, teaching you how to manage emotions, build discipline, and avoid mental traps that derail many traders. There is a dedicated chapter on market manipulation and news events, which will help you recognize how external forces impact price behavior.

As a bonus, you'll also get a collection of ready-to-use resources, including:

Trading checklists, a trading session preparation checklist, and routines. a guide to building your trading journal, and many more.

You will be able to apply this knowledge to any liquid market: stocks, forex, crypto, futures, and more. Enjoy the challenges of trading.

Trading involves significant risk and may not be suitable for all investors. The content of this book is for educational purposes only. Always conduct your own research and consult with your financial advisor before making any trading or investment decisions.

INDEX

1 INTRODUCTION

This book is a collection of the most important professional trading rules and strategies I have learned, analyzed, and applied throughout my trading career, based on more than 12,000 hours of studying charts and trading professionally in the futures, stock, and options markets at the time of this publication.

While this book reveals powerful advanced techniques, it is structured in a way that makes it accessible and easy to follow, regardless of where you are on your trading journey.

I highlight and explain in detail the key differences between widely used, publicly accessible methods and professional trading strategies

This book provides a **step-by-step approach to reading and interpreting charts**, helping you develop a deep understanding of price action and technical analysis, just like professional traders.

I will show you how to use price action to your advantage.

From the very beginning of my career, I had the opportunity to engage with professional traders from various backgrounds and countries, and their invaluable knowledge is also reflected in this book.

This book can be understood as a detailed, practical and technical guide, combined with valuable stories, reflections, and recommendations.

It covers everything you need: core principles, advanced techniques, and detailed guidance on executing trades effectively, along with practical strategies to improve your trading skills every single day.

I will explain advanced techniques used by professional traders and show the exact steps required to execute them, supported by real examples.

In the last chapters, I will focus on some personal experiences, market manipulation, news, and common mistakes. Avoiding these errors will lead to a significant improvement not only in your trading activity but also in your life.

2 THE BIGGEST CHALLENGE

Trading is not only about money. For many professional traders, it represents a fascinating mental and psychological challenge. It is the attempt to decode the language of the market and to understand the hidden rules behind a highly competitive world, the financial market.

Trading is a competition with winners and losers. Whenever one participant makes a profit, another unknown participant or group of participants incurs a loss.

Only the most prepared traders are able to take advantage of the markets.

However, the competition is both external, against other market participants, and internal, against one's own psychology, discipline and strategies.

2.1 COMPETING AGAINST OTHERS

In trading, skill often outweighs luck. The better your strategies and your ability to apply them consistently, the more likely you are to "win" in the market over the long term. This is quite similar to other skill-based competitions, such as sports, chess, or even poker. The difference, however, is that the "competition" is not one-on-one, but rather against a dynamic, constantly changing market environment where participants are anonymous.

2.2 COMPETING AGAINST YOURSELF

One of the most important aspects of trading as a competition is the internal competition you face as a trader. Self-discipline, patience, and the ability to navigate uncertainty and remain rational in the face of market volatility are essential to success. Traders are constantly battling their own psychology, fear, greed, overconfidence, and impatience.

The best traders can remain objective, interpret market signals better than others and act decisively.

SELF-DISCIPLINE, PATIENCE, AND THE ABILITY TO REMAIN RATIONAL IN THE FACE OF MARKET VOLATILITY ARE ESSENTIAL FOR SUCCESS

2.3 PARTICIPANTS OF THE MARKET

Price movements of financial instruments are driven by the buy and sell orders of the various participants in the financial markets. Understanding who these participants are and how they behave is very important for analyzing market dynamics.

There are mainly three groups of market players depending on their trading size and their level of expertise:

Retail investors participate in the markets using personal accounts and typically trade with smaller amounts of capital. Some follow trends, news, and social sentiment, while others rely on knowledge gained from free resources like online courses, books, or trading groups. While some of these sources are valuable, they often lack depth and structure. A common pitfall among retail traders is poor risk management. Many are highly reactive to volatility, becoming emotional or greedy, which leads to poor decisions, such as holding onto losses for too long or exiting profitable trades too early. Additionally, the tools and data available to retail traders are often limited, making it harder to make informed short-term decisions compared to institutional players.

Professional traders typically work with larger positions and handle third-party funds. They possess a deeper understanding of short-term market movements and are usually required by their institutions to follow strict risk management protocols.

They operate between retail and institutional players, capitalizing on the emotional behavior of retail traders while also understanding the strategies and needs of investment firms. By analyzing both sides, they aim to profit from short-term price movements while maintaining a long-term edge.

Investment firms operate with substantial capital but cannot deploy all their funds at once. They often use algorithms to invest large sums in smaller batches. Due to the high volume of their trades, they have the ability to influence market direction, which they may leverage to their advantage.

2.3.1 Liquidity providers

In the stock market, participants can generally be classified into two groups: liquidity providers and liquidity takers, each playing a vital role in the functioning of the market. The balance between these two groups is essential for a healthy and efficient market, particularly in high-volume environments.

Investment firms manage large sums of capital and require sufficient liquidity to execute their trades efficiently. When the buy, they need sellers; when they sell, they need buyers. As such, they rely heavily on the presence of active market participants who can act as counterparties to their transactions - liquidity providers. Without sufficient liquidity, their large trades could cause significant market disruptions or slippage.

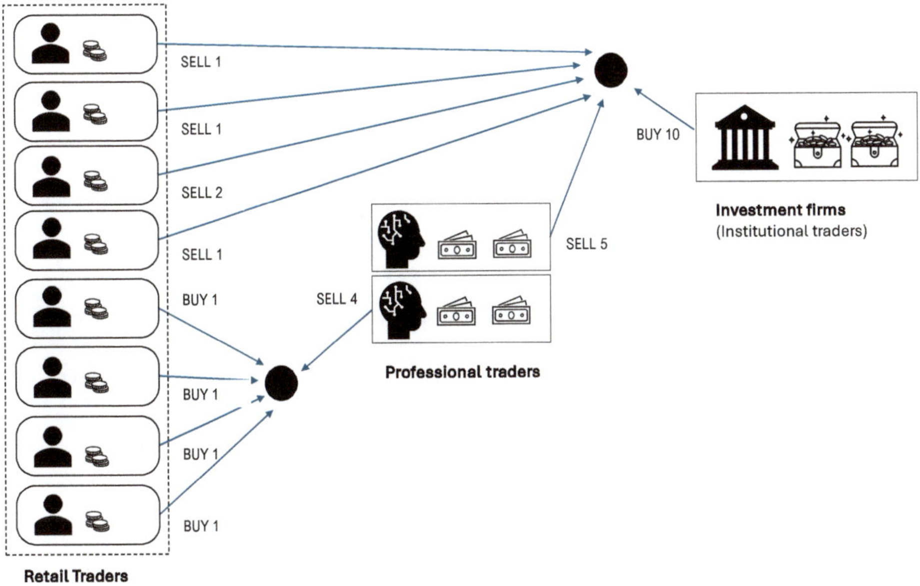

Investment firms need liquidity providers

Interestingly, investment firms can also act as **liquidity providers to each other**, especially when they hold **contrarian views**. For example, one firm may be looking to buy a stock that another is eager to sell, creating natural liquidity within institutional flows.

2.3.2 MARKET MOVERS AND MARKET FOLLOWERS

Market movers are participants who have a significant impact on the overall market direction. Market followers react to the moves initiated by market movers.

Market movers, such as institutional investors, hedge funds, and large corporations, can influence the stock market in several ways:

- By buying or selling a large number of shares, they create significant demand or supply, thereby impacting stock prices.
- They use algorithms to execute large trades in milliseconds, which can create rapid price fluctuations.

The following table shows the main characteristics of the main market participants:

Participant	Traded volume	Market influence	Strategies	Market liquidity
Retail investors	Small	Small or random influence.	They use many different strategies, most of them lack a proven edge, and act emotionally. Their strategies are based on publicly available information sources.	By being active in the markets, they represent a liquidity source for other market participants.
Professional traders	Medium	Sometimes (when there are not many participants in the market).	They use professional trading strategies with an edge in the markets. They are forced to control and minimize losses.	They also deliver liquidity to bigger investment Firms.
Investment firms	Very big	Yes, they induce and influence market movements with their volume.	They used to trade in price zones where the liquidity is high, like Traps (see Traps).	They use the liquidity given by prop traders and retail investors to buy and sell.

2.4 FUNDAMENTAL RULES

Before we get into a deep analysis of charts and how prices move in financial markets, there are some basic but fundamental trading rules that you should always remember, which many retail traders ignore when they are active in the markets. These simple rules are the foundation for any trade.

2.4.1 Buy low and sell high

No matter what timeframe you trade, always make sure that you are buying low and selling high.

It may sound obvious, but it's a rule many retail traders fail to follow, as they often let emotions dictate their decisions.

This principle is no different from the logic you'd apply when buying or selling an everyday asset like a house or a car, waiting for the right price is key to making a profitable deal.

First of all, you need to know what is considered a high price and what is a low price within your chosen timeframe.

This involves:

- Identifying the highest and lowest prices within that period.
- Establishing the average price as a reference point.
- Buying when the price is below the average.
- Selling when the price is above the average.

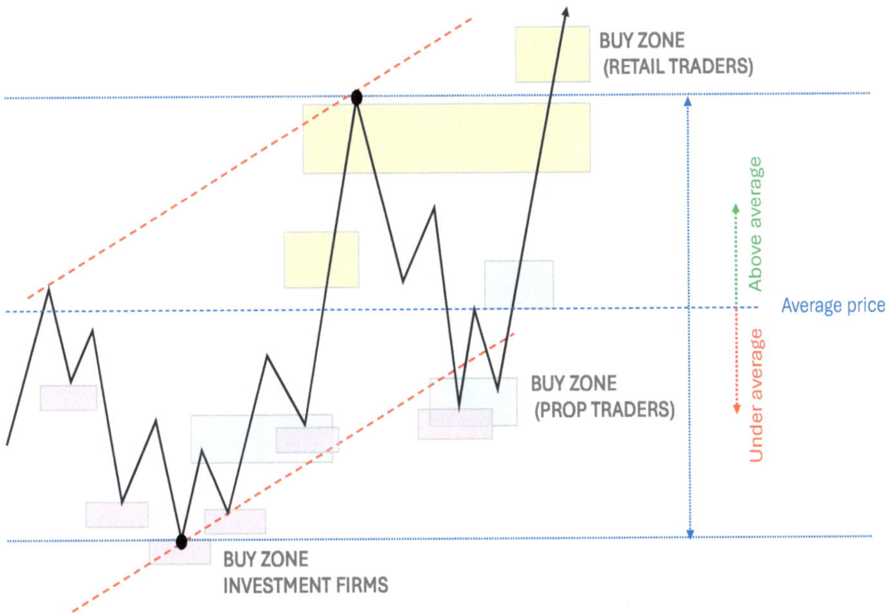

Common Buy zones for different market participants.

In the next chapters we will see how to detect the best buying and selling zones and will explain the best strategies to buy as low as possible and to sell as high as possible.

2.4.2 The advantage of momentum

Momentum in trading refers to the tendency of an asset's price to continue moving in the same direction for a period of time.

By recognizing when momentum is building in a particular direction, you can enter a position early in the trend and ride it for a significant gain. In the coming chapters, we will explore how to identify momentum in the market.

Momentum-driven markets can offer quick and substantial gains. Assets experiencing strong momentum may see rapid price movements, allowing you to capitalize on shorter-term opportunities.

In markets driven by positive news, momentum can push the price higher at a much faster pace compared to a more stagnant environment.

2.4.3 Catalysts for price movements

As your transactions as a trader will last for a short period of time, it is critical that you understand the most essential factors influencing price and the conditions under which prices begin to move.

2.4.3.1 Stop-losses being hit

A stop-loss order is an order which automatically sells or buys a security when it reaches a certain price, thereby limiting potential losses.

When several traders set their stop-losses at similar or predictable levels (for example, immediately below a recent low or above a recent high), these orders accumulate around specific price levels.

When a significant number of stop orders are executed in one direction at the same time, a price move develops as a result of stop-losses being triggered. This behaviour is widespread in financial markets and is commonly referred to as **"stop-loss hunting"**. It can cause strong and rapid price swings, sometimes resulting in price spikes that are difficult for traders to anticipate or respond to in real time.

Professional traders and institutional firms are aware of this behavior and may exploit clustered stop orders by moving the price just below or above certain levels, causing a flood of stop orders to be executed all at once.

As prices plummet, traders with stop-losses in place may see their positions automatically liquidated, accelerating the sell-off. This creates a feedback cycle in which stop-loss orders placed too close to the current price or below specific technical levels are triggered quickly, further driving prices downward.

2.4.3.2 Be aware of the slippage effect

When the price at which an order is executed differs from the price at which it was placed, a phenomenon known as slippage occurs in trading. This is due to market volatility and limited liquidity. If prices fluctuate rapidly or there are not enough buyers or sellers at the desired price, the order is filled at the next available price, resulting in slippage.

For example, if you place a market purchase order at $50 but it executes at $50.20, the $0.20 difference is considered slippage. To reduce slippage, traders often use limit orders, trade during high liquidity periods, and avoid highly volatile market conditions.

Slippage is particularly likely in highly volatile markets, after important news events, or in assets with low trading volume, when price moves can be rapid and irregular.

2.4.3.3 Fear of missing out (FOMO) effect

The Fear of Missing Out (FOMO) is a psychological phenomenon where individuals feel anxious about potentially missing out on an opportunity that others might be enjoying. This feeling leads to strong price reactions due to wrong buying and selling decisions.

Some traders might feel compelled to buy a certain financial product or participate in a new trend just because they fear others will have an advantage or be in the "in-group" if they don't.

2.4.3.4 Margin trading and margin calls

When investors borrow money from a broker to buy stocks (or other assets), using their existing portfolio as collateral, it is known as margin trading.

A margin call occurs when an investor's margin account balance falls below the broker's required minimum due to losses on borrowed funds. In such cases, the investor must deposit additional funds or sell assets to restore the account to the required margin level.

Margin calls from multiple investors can accumulate and intensify market downturns, particularly during periods of high volatility or economic stress. This can trigger a snowball effect, where widespread forced liquidations cause asset prices to fall further, compounding the market decline.

2.5 VOLATILITY

Market volatility can present both opportunities and risks, depending on how traders approach it.

On the positive side, heightened volatility creates more chances for profit, as rapid price swings offer opportunities to buy low and sell high. It also boosts liquidity, making it easier to enter and exit positions. For options traders, increased volatility often means higher premiums, which can be advantageous when selling options.

However, volatility also carries significant risks. Sharp price movements can result in substantial losses, particularly for leveraged traders who may face margin calls. Emotional decision-making becomes a major hurdle as fear and greed can drive impulsive trades during turbulent market conditions.

To navigate volatility successfully, it's essential to apply sound risk management strategies, such as using volatility-based stop-loss orders and maintaining a diversified portfolio, to help protect your capital.

2.6 EVENTS AND NEWS

News plays a crucial role in trading, as it directly influences market sentiment, volatility, and asset prices. Economic reports, earnings releases, interest rate decisions, and geopolitical events can trigger sharp price movements.

Market participants react to news in real-time, adjusting their positions based on the latest information.

Positive news tends to drive prices higher, while negative news can spark sell-offs. High-impact events, such as Federal Reserve statements or major company announcements, often lead to increased trading volume and heightened volatility. A more detailed discussion of the impact of news in trading is covered in Chapter 18.

2.7 MARKET MANIPULATION

The deliberate act of influencing asset prices or the market's behavior for one's own benefit is known as market manipulation.

These practices can involve coordinating trades to confuse market participants, distributing misleading information, or placing fictitious orders (spoofing). Understanding market manipulation is crucial for a number of reasons, particularly for financial professionals, investors and traders.

First, investors can be protected from fraudulent activity by identifying market manipulation. Particularly, retail traders are frequently at risk from fraudulent strategies that distort the actual worth of assets. Without this knowledge, investors might make bad choices based on false signals, which could result in losses.

Second, market fairness and transparency are improved by knowing how manipulation works. Trust is essential to a healthy market; participants must think that prices accurately reflect supply and demand.

Traders and analysts who can identify red flags are better equipped to avoid involvement in unlawful behavior, whether intentional or accidental.

Manipulation can result in large financial losses, mislead investors, and distort fair market conditions. Even though it is prohibited in the majority of countries and markets, it still happens, particularly in places with little regulation.

We'll go into more detail about market manipulation and what manipulation tactics look like in Chapter 17.

3 PROFESSIONAL MARKET ANALYSIS

In this chapter I will show you how professional traders analyze the market and charts to make trading decisions.

Even though each financial instrument is unique, you will be able to apply this understanding to any tradable and liquid financial instrument.

I'll also show you real examples from the futures and stock markets, which I believe are among the most profitable markets to trade.

3.1 ANALYSIS IN 4 STEPS

Before making any trading decision, it is important to answer four basic questions:

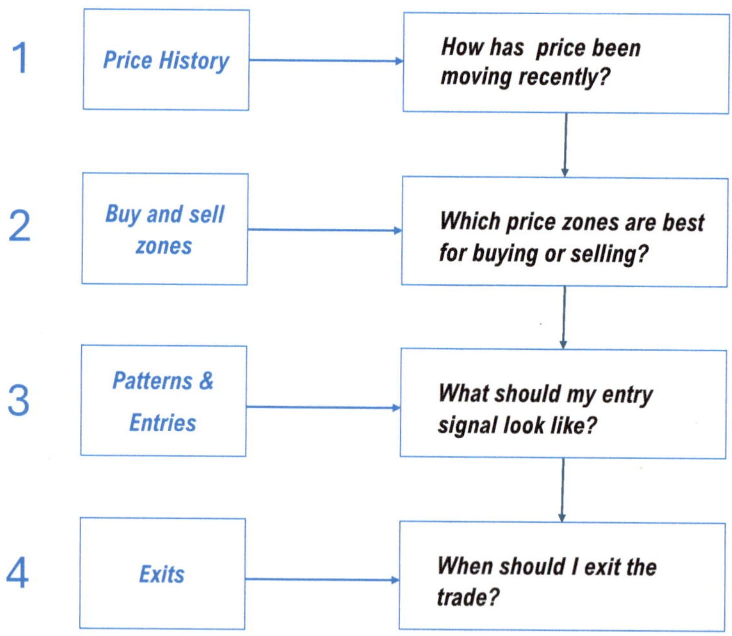

1. *How has the price been moving in the past?*

How does the overall context look like? The answer to this question is called the **"Market Structure".**

In the following example the market structure shows that price is moving sideways, also known as a range-bound market.

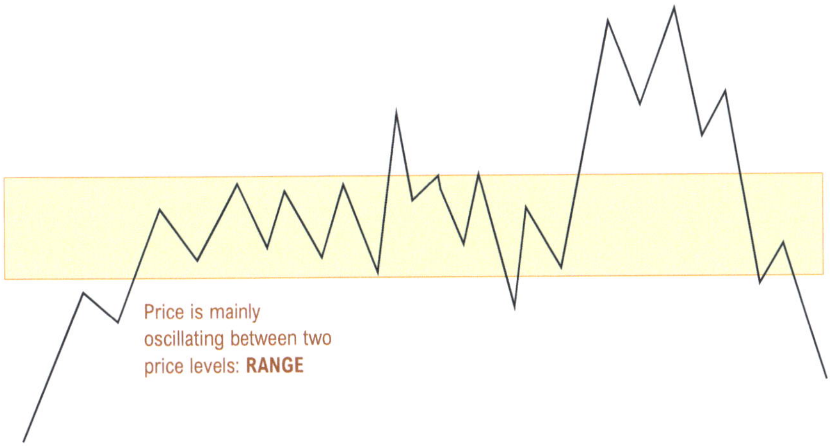

2. *Which price zones are best for buying or selling?*

Using **professional technical analysis**, we will be able to clearly define the optimal zones for entering a trade.

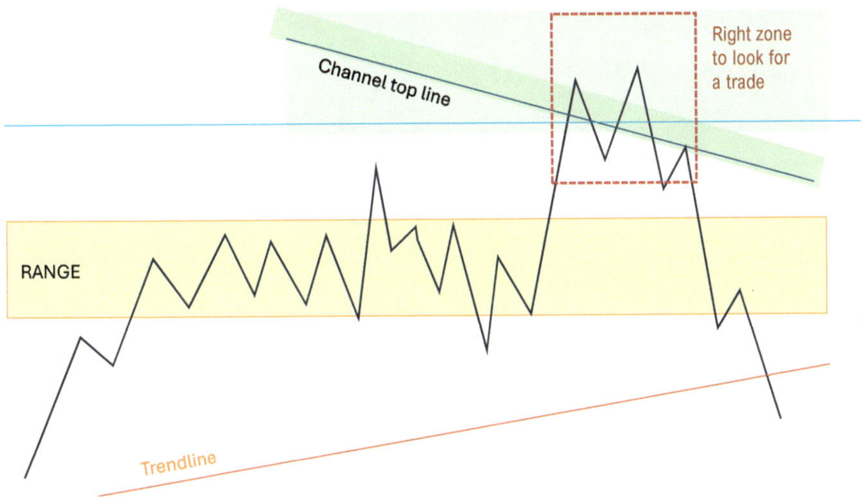

3. *What should my entry signal look like?*

Recognizing the right patterns, along with the right entry signals, will enable you to execute high-probability winning trades. In Chapter 7 "Advanced Patterns", we will develop a detailed list of these patterns with real examples and checklists.

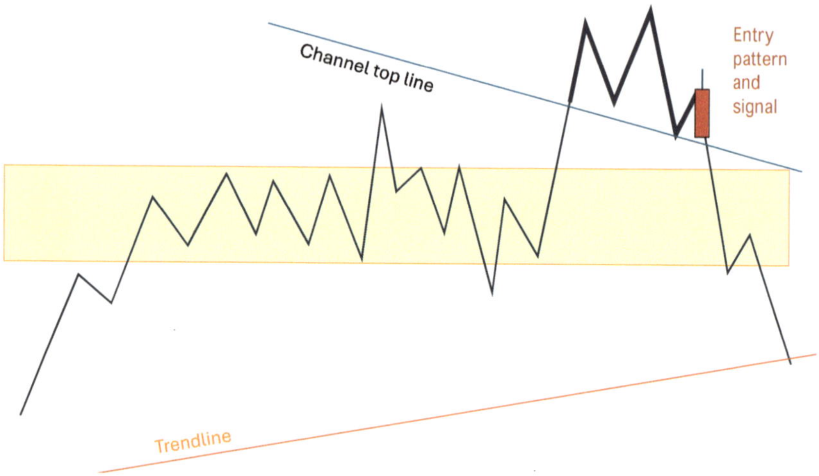

4. *When should I exit the trade?*

What can you expect from the market? What is a realistic target price?

(Chapter 5.4 will be dedicated to target prices.)

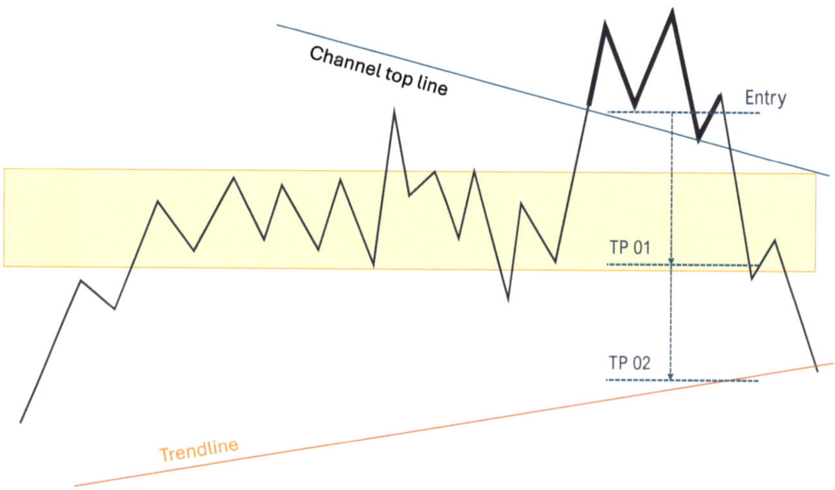

3.2 MARKET STRUCTURE. HOW IS PRICE MOVING?

The first thing you need to analyze is the overall appearance of the market.

Can you recognize a clear movement?

What is the market's main direction?

There are mainly three types of market structures:

- Ranges
- Trending markets (uptrend or downtrend)
- And Choppy markets

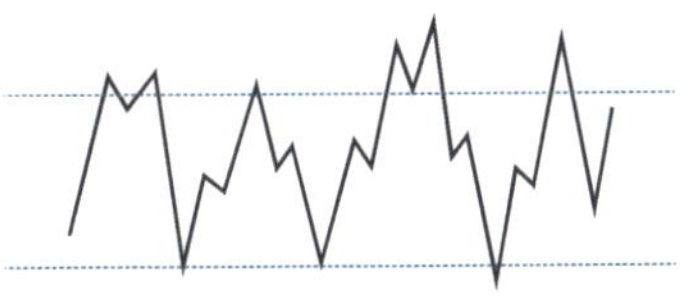

Range market

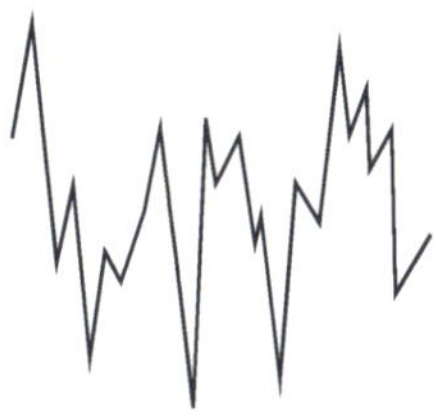

Choppy market

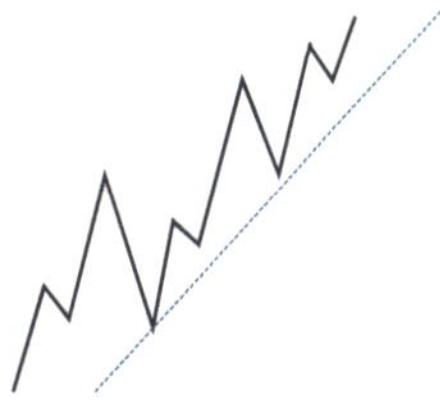

Trending market

Let us investigate them in more detail.

3.2.1 RANGES

In range-bound markets price mainly bounces back and forth between two price levels.

Essentially, this means the asset is trading between a clear support level (the lower boundary) and a resistance level (the upper boundary), without trending in any direction.

Meaning of range markets:

- When range markets are very narrow, and the volume is high, it could indicate that there is a **consensus** about the fair price, with market participants in balance and willing to trade in both directions at that price level.
- Ranges could also mean **accumulation:** when a big investor is sure about the buying price of an asset, she will start to trade big volumes, but

divided into small batches, at a certain price level or price range, often generating ranges in that area (see market movers in Chapter 2.3.2).

- If the price stays within the range, the market remains in a sideways movement, often lacking clear direction. Ranges are also common during periods of **indecision**, low trading volume, or when major news/events haven't yet triggered a significant price move.

3.2.1.1 Important characteristics of Ranges

As ranges can be understood as **fair prices**, participants of the market and investors usually feel comfortable buying at those levels, which leads to the market coming back to those levels sooner or later. They act as **attraction points (magnets)** for the future price.

In the literature you will find the concept "memory of the market", which explains the same phenomenon. This idea is very relevant, and we will see in the next chapters how it can be used to develop high-probability trades.

RANGES ACT AS ATTRACTION POINTS

Example of a Range. BIDU stock 1 min chart. Price coming back to the range.

Example of a Range. Micron stock 2 min chart.

Short trade in a range context. Tesla stock 1 min chart.

3.2.1.2 Range typologies

There are different types of ranges. The most important ones are narrow ranges, wide ranges and triangles.

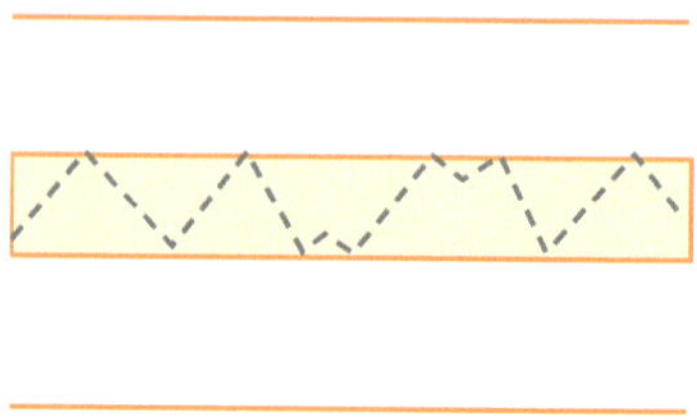

Narrow Range

Narrow ranges are unpredictable and there is no space inside to look for a trade.

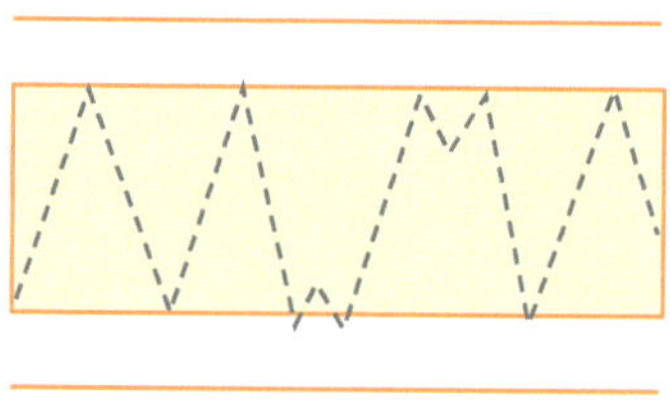

Wide Range

Whereas in wide ranges price can gain momentum in one direction, as there is enough space.

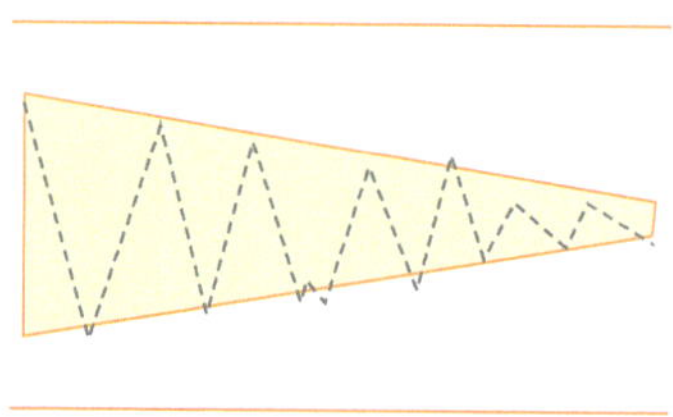

Triangle

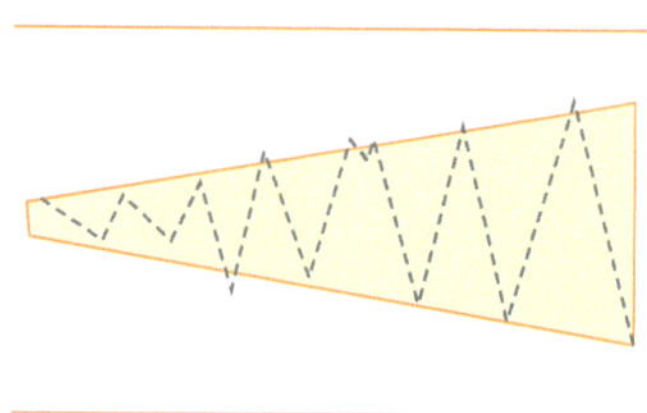

Expanding triangle

Triangles can also be treated as ranges. They can be understood as wide ranges that become narrower over time.

As we will see in Chapter 5.4.1.1, ranges and triangles are attraction areas, and because of this, they can be used as target prices, as price often returns to them.

Example of a range. ES futures contract, 1000tick chart. Price coming back to the range.

Range in ES futures contract, 1000 tick chart.

Range in IONQ stock, 1 min chart.

3.2.2 Trending markets: uptrend or downtrend

A trending market is one that consistently moves in a specific direction, either upward (an uptrend) or downward (a downtrend), over a certain period of time within a given timeframe.

In a trending market, there is a clear and sustained movement in one direction, often driven by strong momentum, investor sentiment, or macroeconomic factors.

In an uptrend (also called a bullish trend), the market forms higher highs (price peaks) and higher lows (price troughs), indicating that buyers are in control and pushing prices upward.

In a downtrend (also called a bearish trend), prices move lower, forming lower highs and lower lows.

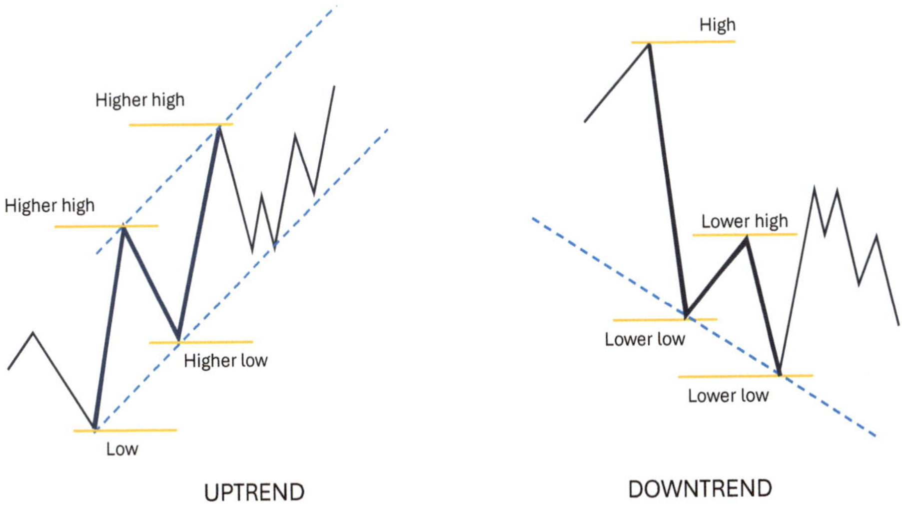

Examples of trending markets

3.2.3 Choppy markets

Choppy markets are undefined and chaotic markets, where it is difficult to find a market structure in the charts. They are characterized by contradictory, erratic and unexpected price movements.

Professional traders avoid these market structures because they lack a clear, exploitable edge, making consistent profitability unlikely.

Choppy markets are very risky, and it is not worth participating in them. Just wait for a better market structure and be patient.

AVOID CHOPPY MARKETS !

Example of a choppy market structure. ES futures contract, 1000 tick chart.

When do choppy markets happen most?

Choppiness typically shows up when:

- Trading volume is very low.
- At the end of the month.
- At the end of the week.
- And also during midday break times (usually between 12 and 1 pm, New York time): during this time professional traders go for lunch and only beginners and retail traders keep on trading. As most of them react emotionally to price movements, the overall market movement may become choppy.

3.2.4 Mixed market structures

It is also possible to see combinations of uptrends, downtrends and ranges coexisting in different timeframes.

A **timeframe** refers to the specific duration or period that each individual price data point (or candle) represents on a chart.

DIFFERENT TIMEFRAMES CAN OFFER DIFFERENT MARKET STRUCTURES

Example of an uptrend in a wide range:

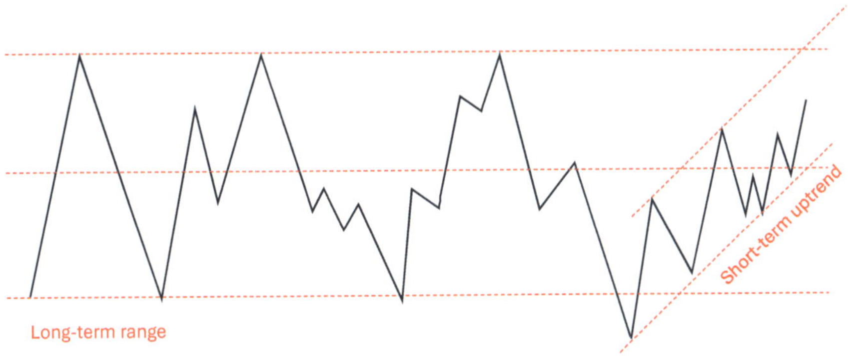

The uptrend will be visible in the 5 min chart

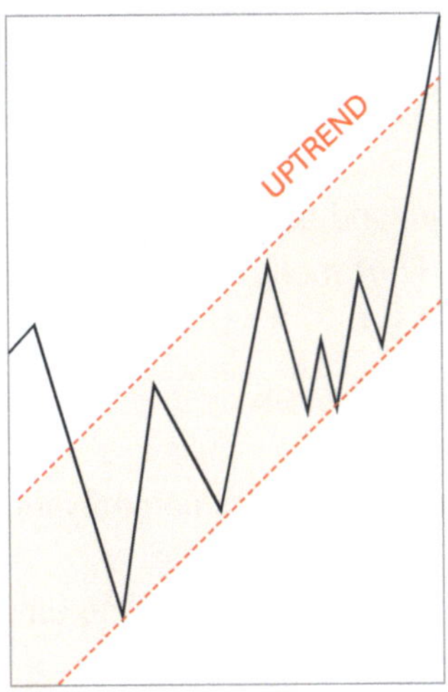

5 min chart.

At the same time a wide range will appear in the higher timeframe, the 15min chart

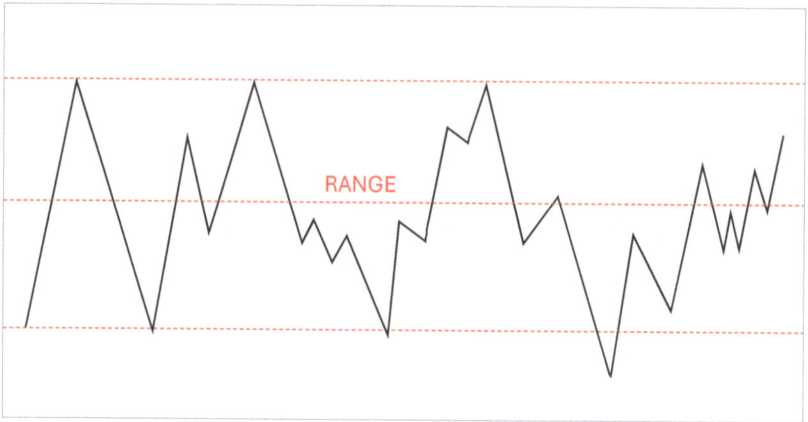

15 min chart.

3.3 SELECTION OF THE RIGHT TIMEFRAME

Your trading style plays a key role in determining the appropriate timeframe. Each trading style involves a different approach to market analysis and holding periods.

3.3.1 ALIGNING TIMEFRAME WITH YOUR TRADING STYLE

If you have the time and discipline to monitor the market constantly, shorter timeframes (1-minute, 5-minute, or 15-minute charts) may suit you.

If you're in it for the long haul and prefer fewer trades with larger profit potential, longer timeframes like weekly or monthly charts might be ideal.

3.3.2 MULTIPLE TIMEFRAME ANALYSIS

Professional traders use **multiple timeframe analysis** to enhance their strategy:

For one trade, professional traders may use three timeframes at the same time:

- The timeframe in which you trade (let us call it **TF**).

- A higher timeframe (let us call it HTF), which is important to understand the overall market structure (including primary trends, attraction points and support and resistance zones, etc.)
- A lower timeframe (let us call it LTF), where optimized trade entries can be identified, allowing for tighter stop-loss placement and an improved risk-reward ratio of your trades. See chapter 9.1.

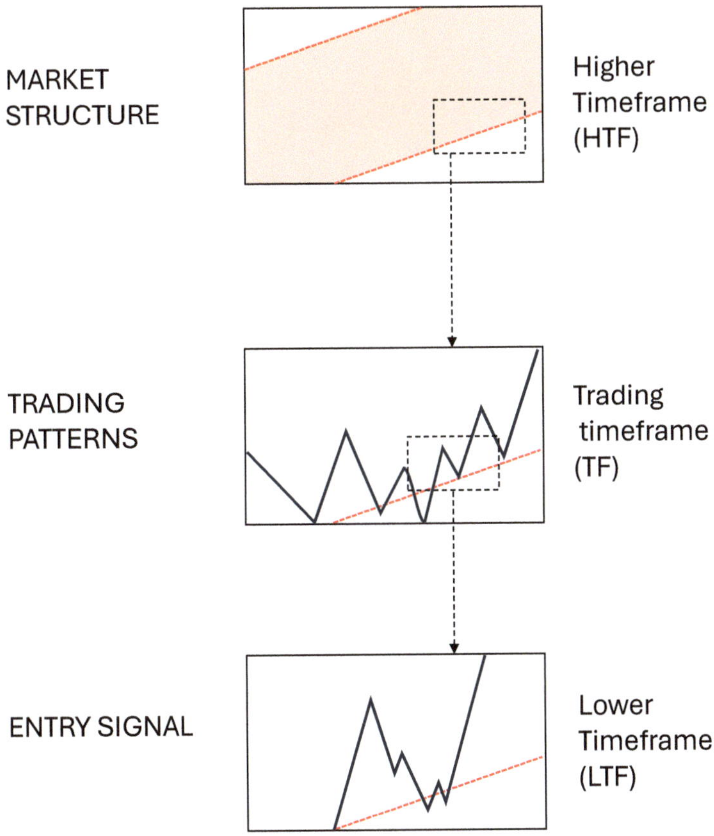

There is a general and quite common rule of thumb which can be applied to interconnect all of them:

The higher timeframe (HTF) should be approximately 6 times bigger than the trading timeframe TF. If you trade in the 5 min chart, you will be using the 30 min chart to analyze the market.

- The lower timeframe (LTF) is around 4 times smaller that the trading timeframe: this means, that the optimization of your entries will be done in the 2 or 1 min chart.

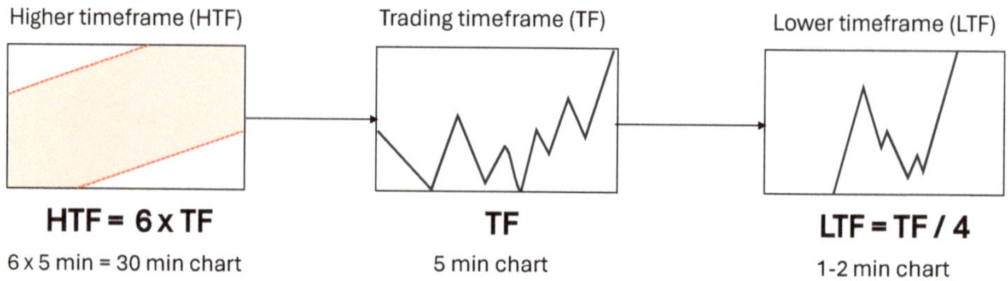

3.3.3 Timeframes and volatility

The volatility of the asset you're trading also plays a role in selecting the timeframe. In volatile markets, shorter timeframes may provide more trading opportunities, but they also come with higher risk.

Longer timeframes (daily or weekly) may be more effective, as price movements are more gradual, and you're less likely to be affected by daily fluctuations or undesirable emotional reactions.

3.3.4 Types of charts

Depending on what financial instrument you are trading, you should setup your charts accordingly. There are many types of charts but I will focus on the best 2 setups/types to trade stocks or futures:

- time based charts
- and tick charts.

3.3.4.1 Time based charts

Time-based charts are the most used type of chart. They provide a visual representation of price data over time, with each candle representing price movement during a specific time interval (e.g., 1 minute, 1 hour, 1 day).

3.3.4.2 Tick based charts/candles

In tick-based charts (tick charts), a candle forms after a set number of trades (also called ticks) occur, regardless of how much time passes. Tick charts print a new candle only after the market completes a specific number of transactions.

Example of a *winning trade (long) in the futures market: Strong candle closing at EMA 21, using a tick chart (1000 ticks). Ninja Trader Platform.*

WHEN TRADING FUTURES (NQ OR ES) I RECOMMEND USING TICK BASED CHARTS

Why?

Tick charts print more candles during high activity and fewer candles when the market is slow. They are better for day trading and scalping because **you see price action** based on real market participation.

TICK CHARTS HELP YOU STAY FOCUS ON REAL PRICE ACTION

Only professional trading platforms offer the option to use and set up tick charts. Ninja Trader is one of them.

4 PROFESSIONAL TECHNICAL ANALYSIS

Once we have identified the existing market structure in the timeframe we are trading, see Chapter 3, it is important to find out which price levels are good to buy and/or sell. Buying and selling zones are dependent on the price behavior in the past. Using professional technical analysis, we will be able to correctly find out the optimal zones to buy and sell.

We will look for historical price levels where the market has reversed multiple times, and based on that, we will concentrate on defining:

- Relevant horizontal support and resistance levels.
- Channels.
- Trendlines.
- Ranges.
- POCs (Points Of Control).

In the literature you will find many other elements and indicators, but the truth is:

You don't need to overcomplicate this analysis. It is enough to focus on the ones mentioned above. Let us take a look in detail at all of them.

4.1 HORIZONTAL SUPPORT AND RESISTANCE LEVELS

A support level is a price where buying pressure is strong enough to prevent the price from falling further.

A resistance level is a price level where selling pressure is strong enough to prevent the price from raising further.

4.1.1 FUNDAMENTAL CHARACTERISTICS OF SUPPORT AND RESISTANCE LEVELS

- **Support and resistance levels are not a line but a zone.**

Support and resistance levels aren't always precise price levels but rather areas or regions where price is likely to encounter buying (support) or selling (resistance) pressure.

Example of a support and resistance zone.

- **Support Turns into Resistance (and vice versa)**

When a support level is broken, it often becomes **resistance**. After a downward breakout, the previously strong support level may act as a ceiling that prices struggle to break above.

Similarly, when a resistance level is broken, it often becomes support. After a breakout to the upside, the previous resistance level may become a floor that prices hold above.

DRAW SUPPORT AND RESISTANCE LEVELS AS ZONES RATHER THAN AS PRECISE LINES.

Example of a resistance level turning support.

- **Further characteristics of support and resistance levels:**
  - If price repeatedly tests a support/resistance level, it becomes weaker and more likely to break.
  - When the price breaks through a resistance level with significant momentum, it can signal the start of a new trend.
  - Support and resistance levels on higher timeframes (like the daily, weekly, or monthly charts) are often stronger and more significant.
  - Support and resistance levels on shorter timeframes (like the 1-minute or 2-minute charts) may be less reliable since they can be more easily broken due to market noise.
  - False Breakouts: Sometimes, price can break above resistance or below support only to reverse quickly, creating a "false breakout", see Chapter 6.4.4.

SUPPORT TURNS INTO RESISTANCE (AND VICE VERSA)

4.2 CHANNELS

In trending markets (uptrend or downtrend) the price of an asset is frequently embedded in channels.

The idea of the price moving inside a channel is simple. The key to leveraging channels effectively lies in knowing how to draw them logically and accurately.

PROFESSIONAL TRADERS DRAW CHANNELS IN A DIFFERENT WAY

4.2.1 THE WRONG METHOD OF DRAWING CHANNELS

Most retail traders draw channels in search of one that best fits the existing market swings, as illustrated in the following image.

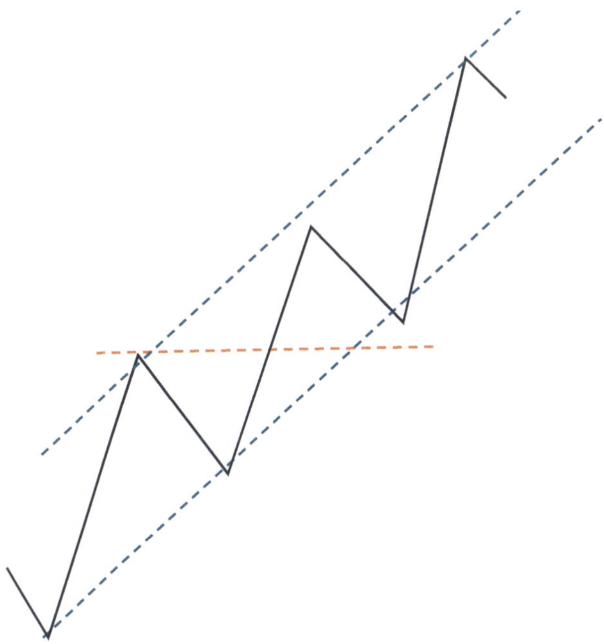

Wrong method of drawing channels.

The problem with this method is that you need to wait for multiple bounces off the channel to recognize and confirm it. And waiting too long might result in entering a trade too late, by which time the trend momentum could already be over.

4.2.2 THE PROFESSIONAL METHOD OF DRAWING CHANNELS

Professional traders draw channels in a different way.

The goal is to identify potential channels early and anticipate their structure, allowing you to take advantage of the existing price momentum before it fully develops.

These are the necessary steps to draw and anticipate a channel in an uptrend as professional traders do:

STEP 1: How to draw the top line (L1) of a channel in an uptrend.

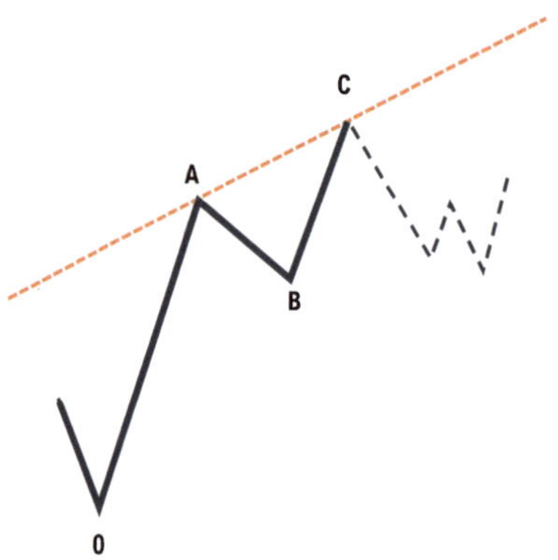

L1
Draw a line (L1)
through A and C:
A: swing high (candle high)
C: higher swing high (candle high)

STEP 2: How to draw the bottom line (L2) of a channel in an uptrend.

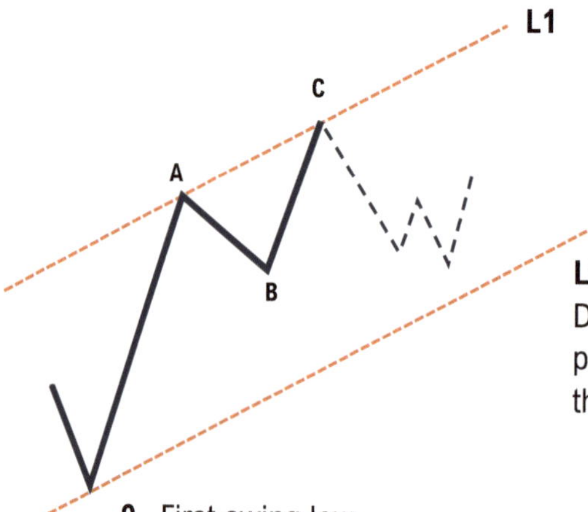

L2
Draw a line (L2)
parallel to L1
through point O

0 First swing low

STEP 3: This step is important! How is point 0 determined?

Point 0, through which the bottom line of the channel is drawn, differs depending on which candlestick pattern forms the first swing low. There are two different cases:

Case 1: Pin bar

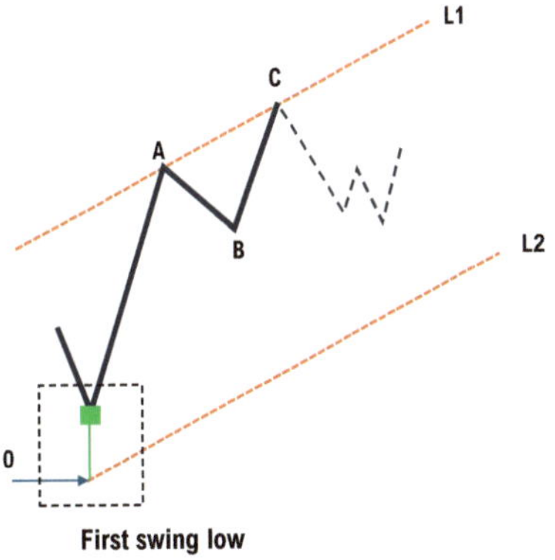

Case 2: Red + green candle

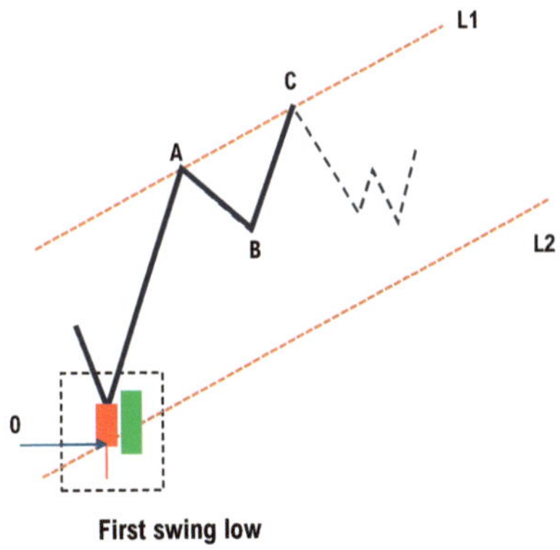

THIS DETAIL IS IMPORTANT AND MAKES THE DIFFERENCE!

Let us zoom in:

- **Case 1:** When the swing low is formed by a pin bar candle, the bottom line (L2) of the channel must be drawn through the candle low of the pin bar candle.

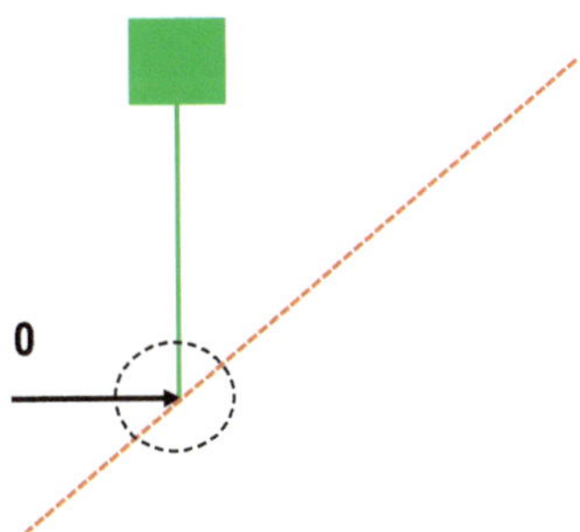

- **Case 2:** When a swing low is formed by two candles (a red and a green candle), the bottom line of the channel (L2) must be drawn through the closing price of the red candle.

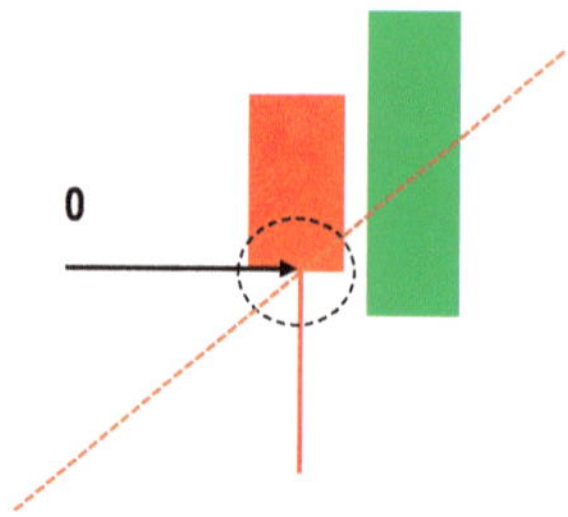

Examples:

Example of an uptrend channel. Micron stock. 1 min chart.

Example of a downtrend channel. ES futures contract, 1000 tick chart.

4.3 TRENDLINES: THE PROFESSIONAL METHOD

Similar to channels, there is a professional method for drawing trendlines (TL), which differs from the methods commonly taught on mainstream educational platforms.

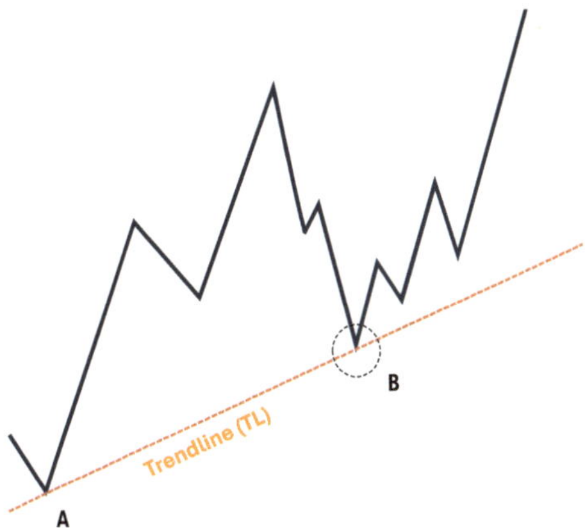

I will show you how to draw trendlines in both, uptrends and downtrends as professionals do.

The important part here is how to correctly select the exact points, A and B.

1. **Drawing a trendline (TL) in an uptrend**
   In an uptrend, the trendline is formed by connecting **A** and **B**, with **A** being the lowest point of the first swing low. And **B (this is important and makes the difference!)** will be determined as follows:

   Case 1: When the swing low (B) is formed by a green pin bar candle, the TL must be drawn through the candle low of the pin bar candle.

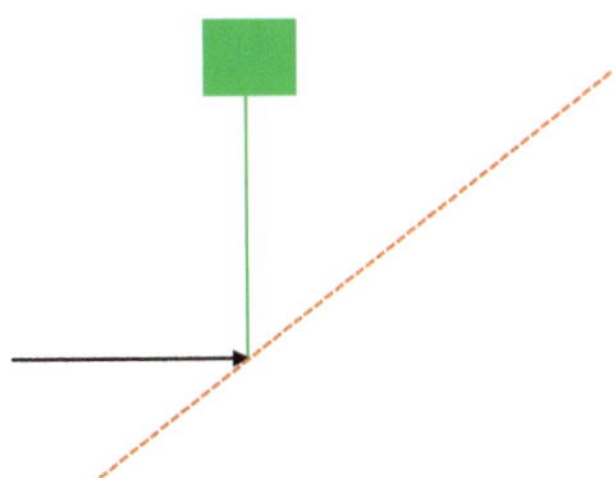

Case 1

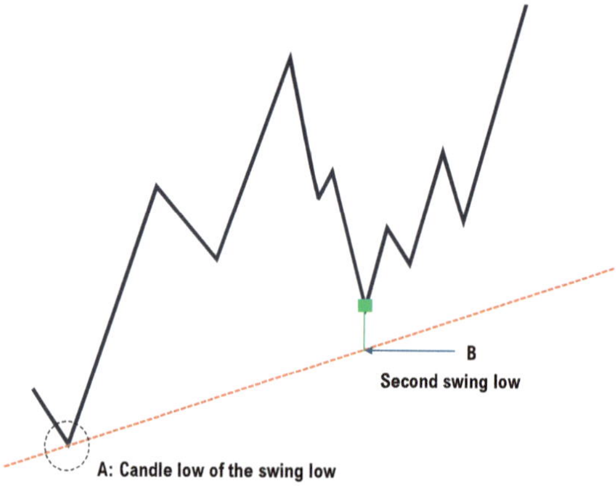

Example of a trendline in an uptrend with a second swing low formed by a green pin bar candle.

Case 2: When the swing low is formed by two candles (a red and a green one), the TL must be drawn passing through the candle close of the red candle, like this:

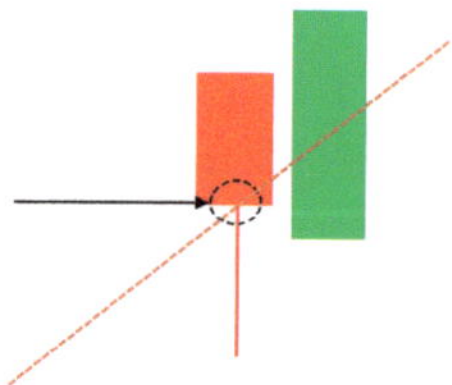

Case 2

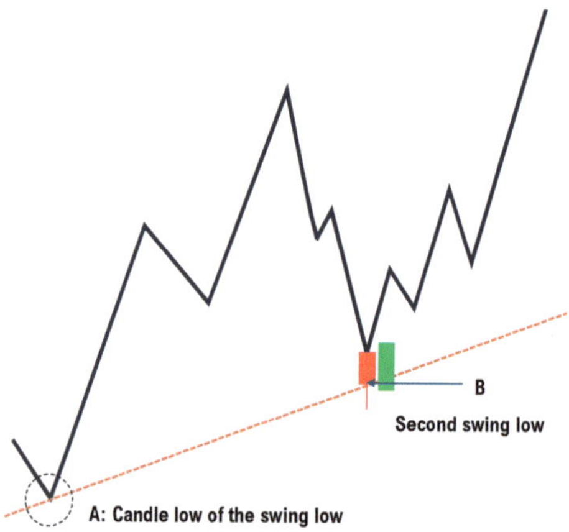

Example of a trendline in an uptrend with a second swing low formed by two candles (a red and a green one).

2. Drawing a trendline (TL) in a downtrend

Case 1: When the second swing high is formed by a red pin bar candle, the TL must be drawn through the candle high of the pin bar candle.

Case 1

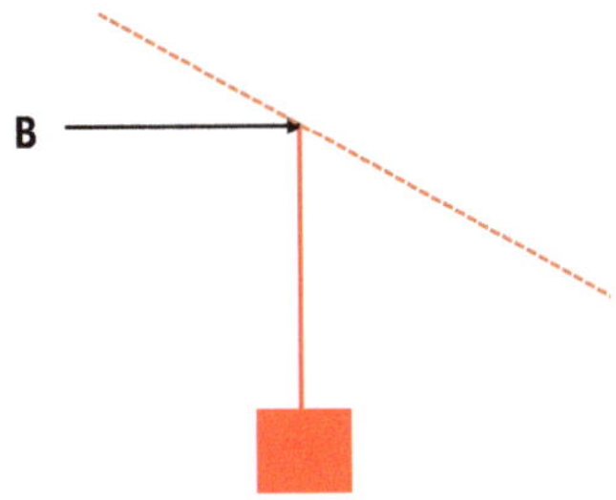

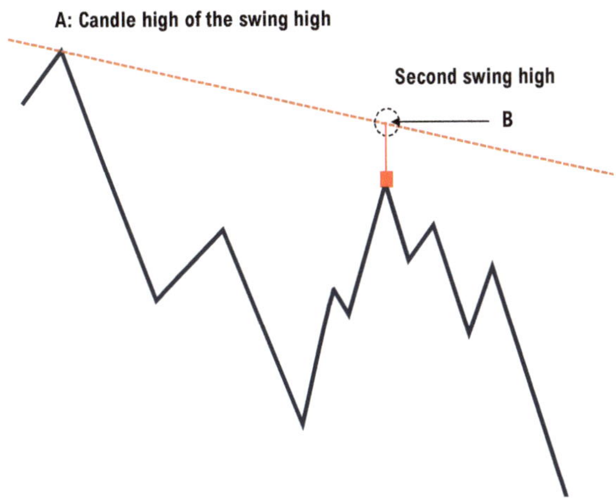

Example of a trendline in a downtrend with a second swing high formed by a red pin bar candle.

Case 2: When the second swing high is formed by two candles (a green candle followed by a red one), the TL should be drawn through the closing price of the green candle, and not through the candle high as many traders mistakenly believe.

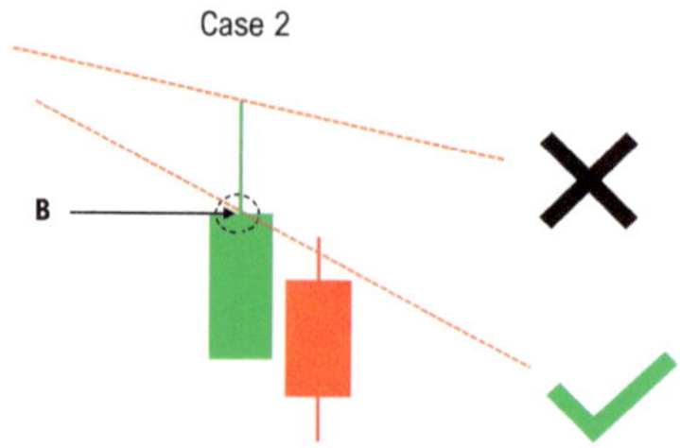

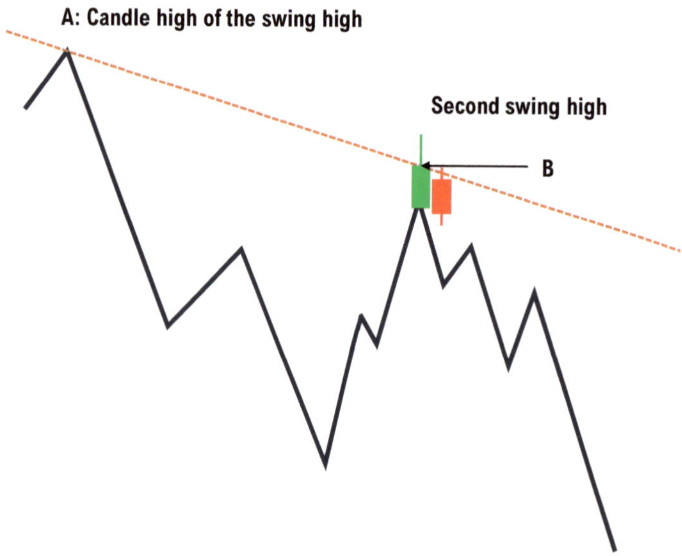

Example of a trendline in a downtrend with a second swing high formed by two candles (a green and a red one).

Example of a trendline in a 1000 tick chart (ES futures contract).

Important characteristics of trendlines:

- Trendlines are strong support and resistance levels.
- You *just need* two major swings to define the trendline: don't wait for more confirmations, as it can be too late. The 3rd bounce of a trendline is a good spot to look for a trade.
- Trendlines can also become support, after being resistant areas and vice versa.

Example of 2 trendlines, ES futures contract. 1000 tick chart.

Example of a trendline through the candle high of a pin bar candle, which becomes a resistance level after being a support level.

4.4 CONFLUENCE IS KEY IN TRADING

Confluence in trading refers to the idea of multiple technical indicators, price action patterns, or key levels aligning at the same point or over a certain area, suggesting a higher probability that a particular market event will occur.

Look for confluence between a higher timeframe trend and lower timeframe setups.

4.4.1 WHY DOES CONFLUENCE WORK?

When various signals or factors converge (or "confluent"), it provides stronger confirmation for a high probability trade setup, **as many traders, using different converging strategies, are going to be looking at the same chart spot to place their trades.**

4.4.2 CONFLUENCE AND CONFIDENCE

The more factors align at a given point, the stronger the signal becomes, and the higher the probability of the trade working out.

Confluence will increase your chances of making successful trades, while also improving the overall confidence and precision in your decision-making process.

Confluence level: 1 Resistance level, 1 channel top line, 2 Trendlines and VWAP and EMA21 indicators converging at the same point. IONQ stock 2min char.

Regardless of the high probability of success when using trading strategies based on confluence, always use stop-loss orders and adjust your position size according to your risk tolerance.

Remember, even the best-looking trades and strategies fail at some point.

LOOK ALWAYS FOR STRONG CONFLUENCE ZONES TO PLACE YOUR TRADES

High confluence level: 1 resistance level, 1 channel bottom line and 3 trendlines, EMA 21 and a strong signal candle. ES futures contract, 1000 tick chart.

WAIT FOR MULTIPLE SIGNALS TO ALIGN AND OVERLAP

Example of confluence at swing low to define a target price. RSI < 10 confirms the target price at $99.20.

Zones, where different trendlines or channel lines intersect, combined with the right entry signals and other parameters, for instance, RSI >80 for a short position or RSI < 20 for a long position, are the best areas to place a trade.

Confluence is when different ways of analyzing a chart lead to the same buy or sell decision

4.4.3 Confluence to define entry and exit levels

Confluence can be used either to define good entry zones or to find good target levels. It works in both directions.

Example of a target price at confluence level. Micron stock, 1min chart.

4.4.4 Why good-looking trades are the riskiest ?

Trades that appear exceptionally promising, those with high confluence and an obvious setup, are often the riskiest. Their appeal attracts a large number of traders, creating ideal conditions for market traps.

When too many participants take the same position, institutions and market makers capitalize on this by driving the price in the opposite direction. Picture-perfect breakouts frequently turn into bull or bear traps, where price reverses sharply after luring traders in. These engineered moves allow big players to absorb liquidity from retail traders.

Obvious setups also lead to clustered stop-losses, which, when triggered, fuel rapid and aggressive price swings in the opposite direction. This stop-hunting behavior further reinforces the cycle, shaking out retail traders before the market resumes its true direction.

GOOD-LOOKING TRADES OFTEN FAIL MORE SHARPLY THAN OTHERS,

NEVER EVER MOVE YOUR STOP-LOSS !

4.5 INDICATORS

Technical indicators are divided into leading and lagging indicators.

These are the main differences between them:

Leading indicators:

- They are based on current data.
- They offer information about future price movements, providing **early signals** of potential trend changes.

Lagging indicators:

- They are based on past price data.
- They provide entry **signals after a move has occurred (too late)**
- They can be used as a further confirmation, but not as an entry signal.

4.5.1 COMBINING LAGGING AND LEADING INDICATORS: LESS IS MORE

Many professional traders combine both lagging and leading indicators to create a more robust trading strategy. The key idea is to use leading indicators to get early signals and lagging indicators to confirm those signals.

Many trading platforms offer hundreds of them. Keep your trading as simple as possible.

IT IS NOT NECESSARY TO KNOW AND USE ALL INDICATORS

In this book, I will focus on the most commonly used indicators among prop traders, as they are more than sufficient for making informed trading decisions:

Leading indicators

- Price
- Volume
- Volume profile
- POC

Lagging indicators

- RSI
- Bollinger Bands
- Volume profile
- VWAP
- EMA 21

4.5.2 Leading Indicators

4.5.2.1 Price

Price is the most important and reliable leading indicator. Unlike other indicators that are derived from price data, the price itself **provides the most direct information about the market's current condition** and potential future direction.

THE PRICE ITSELF IS THE BEST INDICATOR

In essence, price action traders use the raw price data - such as open, high, low and close prices - to make trading decisions.

You don't have to rely on technical indicators or other fancy charting tools, if you understand the language of price action.

Price action itself, the analysis of historical price movements, provides early warning signals of trend changes and deliver necessary clues about future price movements.

4.5.2.2 Volume

Volume is the number of shares, contracts, or lots traded during a given period. It is one of the most important indicators because it provides insight into the strength or weakness of a price movement. Higher volume typically signals greater market interest and conviction behind a price move, while lower volume may indicate a lack of commitment or uncertainty.

However, it's important to remember that volume can be manipulated. Therefore, it should not be used in isolation, but rather as a complementary tool alongside price action and other indicators. Volume adds an extra layer of confirmation to your trade setups.

Example:

> *If price moves strongly (either upward or downward) and is accompanied by high volume, it suggests strong conviction behind the move. High volume confirms, with a high probability, that the price movement is genuine and not merely a temporary fluctuation.*

4.5.2.3 *Volume profile*

Volume Profile is a powerful tool that shows the distribution of trading volume at different price levels over a specified period of time. Unlike traditional volume indicators, which typically show volume by time (i.e. the number of shares or contracts traded during a given time interval on a time axis), the volume profile shows volume on a price axis.

It is useful to identify price levels with high and low trading activity, revealing important support and resistance areas.

Each horizontal bar shows the traded volume at that price level.

Example of the volume profile indicator and POC.

4.5.2.4 *Point of Control (POC)*

The point of control, often abbreviated as POC, represents the price level at which the most trading activity (i.e. the highest volume of trades) occurred during a specified period, typically within a trading session or a specified period of market activity. It is the price level at which the market reached the most agreement or consensus in terms of trading activity, where buyers and sellers come together in significant numbers, often indicating a balance between supply and demand. Traders view this level as a reflection of where the market perceives fair value to be at the time.

Value Area (VA)

In Market Profile analysis, the area around the POC is referred to as the "Value Area". It typically encompasses a range of prices where a significant proportion of the trading volume occurred. This area is often seen as a range within which the market considers the price of the instrument to be relatively fair for the session.

Market Profile is a unique and visual approach to analyzing price and volume data in trading.

It helps traders understand how price and volume are distributed throughout the trading day. With this indicator you can quickly identify price areas with high and low trading activity.

The shape and position of the market profile can provide valuable insights into market sentiment.

- A balanced profile with a well-defined POC typically indicates a market in equilibrium.
- In contrast, an elongated profile may suggest a trending market.

4.5.3 LAGGING INDICATORS

Lagging indicators, as the name suggests, follow price action. They are reactive tools, meaning they are based on past price data and therefore they tend to offer **delayed** signals. By the time they confirm a trend, a significant part of the move may already have occurred.

Lagging indicators are excellent for confirming trends and providing signals once a trend is established, making them less ideal for early entries.

LAGGING INDICATORS ARE NOT GOOD FOR EARLY ENTRIES, USE THEM AS A CONFIRMATION

4.5.3.1 RSI

Relative Strength Index measures the strength and speed of price movements. It can indicate whether an asset is overbought (above 70) or oversold (below 30), which often signals a potential reversal.

RSI is one of the best lagging indicators for confirming trade opportunities.

When the RSI falls below 10, there might be interesting to look for a long trade.

RSI values above 80 signal a highly overbought market and a good spot to be looking for a short position.

Example of the RSI indicator in undersold area. RSI < 10.

4.5.3.2 Bollinger Bands

This indicator consists of a middle band, which is a simple moving average (SMA), and two outer bands that represent standard deviations of price movement from the middle band.

The middle band is typically a 20-period simple moving average (SMA).

The upper band is calculated by adding a specified number of standard deviations (usually 2) to the middle band (SMA).

The lower band is calculated by subtracting a specified number of standard deviations (usually 2) from the middle band (SMA).

The distance between the bands is an important aspect of interpreting Bollinger Bands, as it gives traders a sense of market volatility.

Tightening bands often precede significant price movements (breakouts), while wide bands indicate more volatile conditions.

BOLINGER BANDS WORK WELL IN RANGES AND CAN BE USED TO SET RELIABLE TARGET PRICES

Bollinger Bands. Nvidia stock 1min chart.

BOLINGER BANDS WORKS BEST AT HIGHER TIMEFRAMES

4.5.3.3 VWAP

VWAP provides the average price of an asset, weighted by the volume traded at each price level over a specific period.

It is calculated by taking the total value of all trades in a given period (price multiplied by volume) and dividing it by the total volume for that period.

$$VWAP = \frac{\sum(Price \times Volume)}{\sum Volume}$$

Where:

- **Price** is the price at each trade.
- **Volume** is the number of shares or contracts traded at each price.

is one of the most important indicators.

VWAP IS USED PRIMARILY FOR INTRADAY TRADING

VWAP is generally used for intraday trading, particularly on shorter timeframes like 2-minute, 5-minute, or 15-minute charts. Since it resets every day, it is not typically used for longer-term analysis,

VWAP can be used as an attraction level for the price of an asset and can be used as a target price.

Example of the VWAP indicator. ES futures contract. 1000 tick chart.

4.5.3.4 EMA 21 (Exponential moving average 21)

EMA 21 is the most important indicator in trading, as it can be used as a price reference, where price always comes back to. It gives an idea of the average price over the past 21 candles.

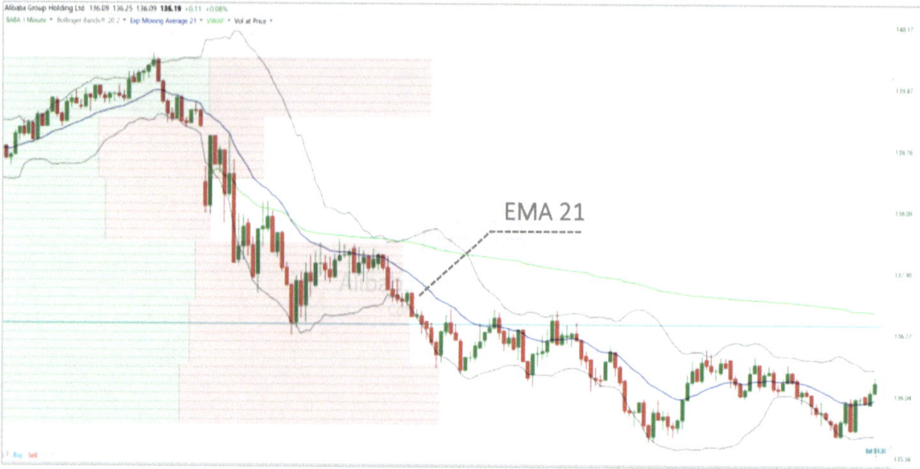

Example of the exponential moving average 21 (EMA 21) indicator. BABA stock, in 1 min chart.

THE EMA21 IS THE REFERENCE FOR MOST PROFESSIONAL TRADERS

EMA 21 can be used to determine if a trend is in place, as explained in Chapter 6.3.

IF PRICE BOUNCES OFF THE EMA 21 WITH STRENGTH, YOU MIGHT HAVE FOUND THE BEGINNING OF A TREND

4.5.3.5 What about Fibonacci?

Fibonacci retracement levels are widely used in trading. Fibonacci levels (like 23.6%, 38.2%, 50%, 61.8%, 78.6%) help validate existing support and resistance levels rather than generating entry signals on their own.

If price reacts at a Fibonacci level where other support/resistance exists, and multiple elements line up, the setup becomes more reliable.

Example of a Strong Confluence Setup, see conditions:

1. *Price pulls back to 61.8% Fibonacci retracement.*
2. *The same level is a major support zone.*
3. *200 EMA is right at that level.*
4. *A bullish engulfing candle forms.*
5. *Volume spikes, confirming buyers stepping in.*

4.5.3.6 ATR14: Volatility-Based Stop-losses

Average True Range (ATR) is a very important indicator which is mainly used to calculate the position of stop-loss orders. It is a popular volatility indicator that measures the average range of price movement over a defined period, which is usually 14 candles (ATR 14). Using ATR can help you adjust your stop-loss based on current market conditions. If volatility is high, you may need to widen your stop; if volatility is low, you might tighten it. Because it's based on historical price action, it is considered a lagging indicator.

Using ATR-based stops helps avoid being stopped out by short-term spikes or "noise" while still protecting you from larger market moves that go against you.

DEFINE VOLATILITY-BASED STOPS USING ATR 14

In Chapter 9.4. I will show you an example of how to calculate your stop-losses based on ATR14.

5 PRICE ACTION: THE MATHEMATICAL VIEW

Price action traders believe that all essential trading information is reflected in the price movement of an asset.

Price action refers to the study and analysis of price movements on a chart, typically without relying on additional indicators or oscillators.

Traders who use price action focus on interpreting the raw price data, including specific candlestick formations, patterns, trends, key support and resistance levels and other price-related signals to determine entry and exit points for their trades.

By studying how price behaves under various market conditions, it is possible to anticipate future price movements. This approach is based on understanding the interaction between buyers and sellers, as every price movement reflects the collective psychology and decisions of all market participants.

ALL ESSENTIAL TRADING INFORMATION IS REFLECTED IN THE PRICE MOVEMENT: PRICE ACTION

5.1 FRACTALS

The theory of fractals in technical analysis suggests that financial markets, while inherently chaotic, exhibit recurring patterns that are not purely random. This concept stems from the broader mathematical theory of fractals, first introduced by Benoit Mandelbrot in the 1970s.

Mandelbrot's research demonstrated that many natural phenomena exhibit fractal characteristics, including self-similarity across different scales, where the same patterns repeat at various sizes and frequencies within a larger structure. He applied this concept to market analysis, highlighting how price movements can display fractal-like behaviour.

In the following examples you can clearly see the same fractal pattern (order) repeating at different timeframes

NQ 1min chart. 123 pattern followed by a narrow channel.

NQ 15min chart. 123 pattern followed by a narrow channel.

FLUCTUATIONS IN ASSET PRICES HAVE A FRACTAL BEHAVIOUR WITH REPEATING PATTERNS IN DIFFERENT TIMEFRAMES

5.2 MEASURED MOVES: THE REPEATING ORDER

If price movements of financial instruments have a fractal behaviour, the question is:

Is there any identifiable order in charts, that can be easily recognized? Can this order be used to make trading decisions?

The answer is yes, price movements are composed of **Measured Moves.**

The basic idea behind a measured move is that the market is very likely to travel the same distance in the same direction as it did during a previous move.

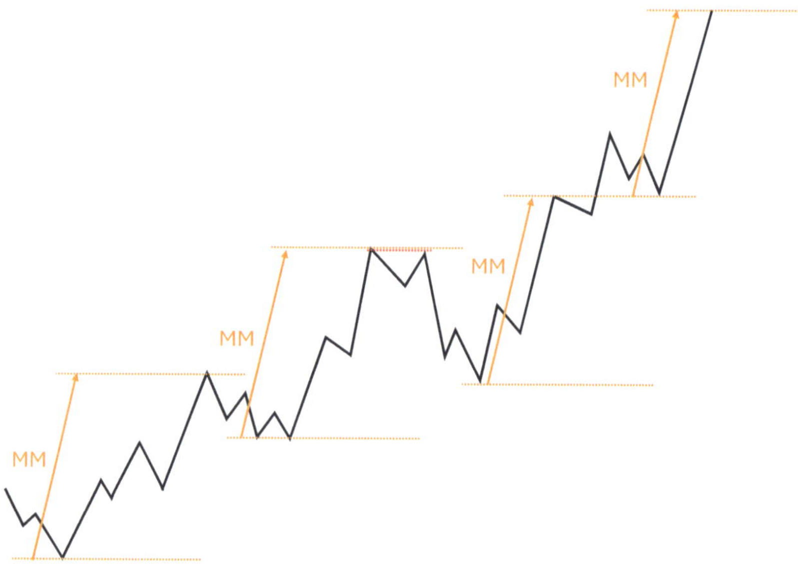

5.2.1 THE IMPORTANCE OF MEASURED MOVES

Measured moves are commonly used to forecast price targets, based on historical price action. By projecting the length of a previous price move in the same direction, you can estimate where the market might move next. Many professional traders anticipate that the next leg of the price movement will reach this projected level, making it a useful reference for setting target prices.

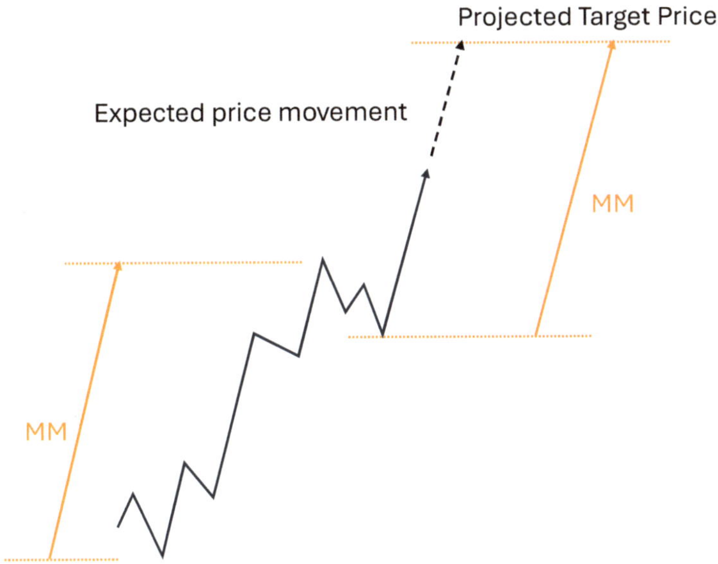

Using measured moves to predict potential target prices

> ***PRICE MOVEMENTS IN THE SAME DIRECTION WITH THE SAME SIZE ARE CALLED MEASURED MOVES***

5.2.2 FUNDAMENTAL CHARACTERISTICS

1. Measured moves appear in all timeframes.
2. Every leg or measured move can also be subdivided into smaller measured moves (as they are based on a fractal behavior). There are two typical patterns:
    a. Two-legged structures with equal sizes.
    b. Three-legged structures:
        i. where the first and third legs have the same size.
        ii. and the second leg is usually bigger.

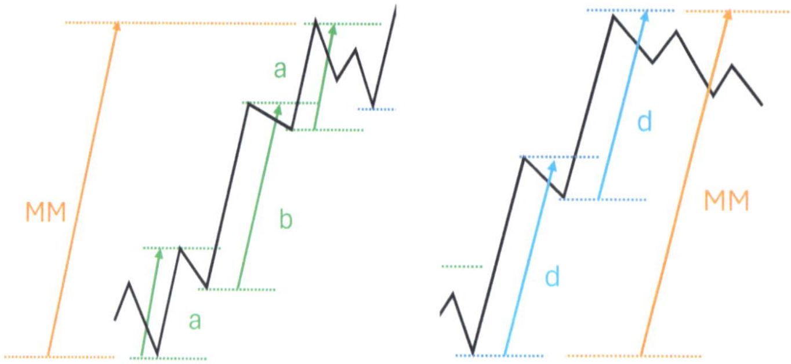

3. Retracements (short-term movements against the trend) can also be composed of measured moves. They can contain 1, 2 or 3 legs.

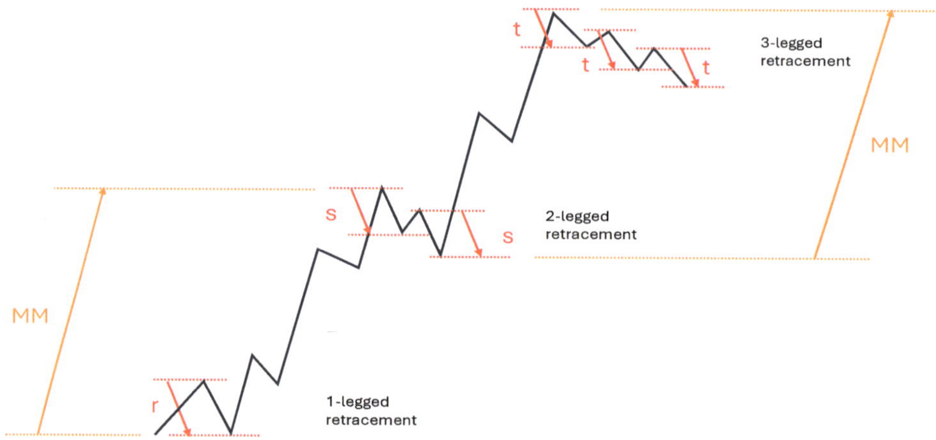

4. The same measured move can repeat 4 or 5 times if the momentum is very strong.

Example of 4 measured moves as end of the movement.

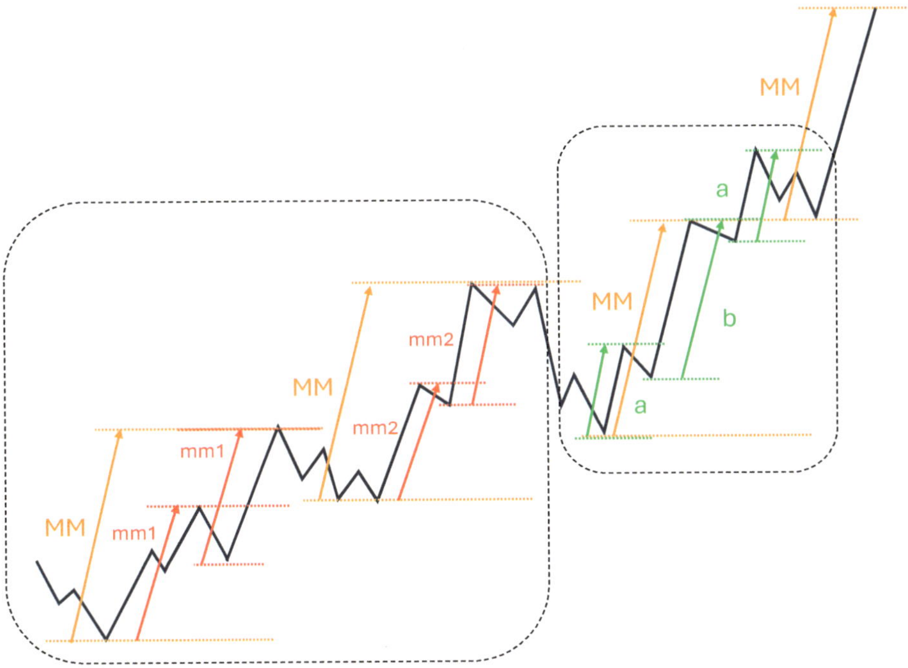

5.2.3 How to use measured moves

- **Identify the first leg of the move:**

Look for an initial price movement, that forms a "leg". This phase could be either upward or downward, and is typically measured (in an uptrend) from the starting point (swing low) to the peak (swing high) of the move.

- **Measure the distance:**

The distance of the first leg is the measured move. For example, if the market moves 50 points upward, that distance represents the measured move.

- **Identify the next swing low and project the measured move from there:**

Next, project the price movement in the same direction from the beginning of the following leg. If the market previously moved 50 points upward, you can expect the price to move approximately 50 points higher from the next swing low. This projected price level can be used as a potential target price.

- **Price Target or potential resistance levels:**

Measured moves can act as a potential resistance or support level, depending on the direction of the move. They are commonly used as reference points for setting target prices.

Measured moves in Micron Stock 2 mins chart, acting as a resistance and support level.

MEASURED MOVES ARE ALSO STRONG SUPPORT AND RESISTANCE LEVELS

Measured moves in Tesla Stock 1 min chart.

5.2.4 How many measured moves are typical

The number of **measured moves** you can expect depends on the trend, market conditions, and the timeframe being analyzed.

- Strong trends: 4 to 5 measured moves.
- Normal trends: Typically, after 3 measured moves, the probability of a trend reversal increases.

5.3 PRICE MOVEMENTS IN CHANNELS AND RANGES

Another geometrical aspect of price movements is that they are generally embedded in **channels** or **ranges**, which may, in turn, be nested within larger channels or ranges, as explained in Chapter 3.2.4.

Always try to answer the following question:

Which already existing channel or pattern is influencing the current price movement?

It is worth looking at a higher timeframe to understand the whole picture.

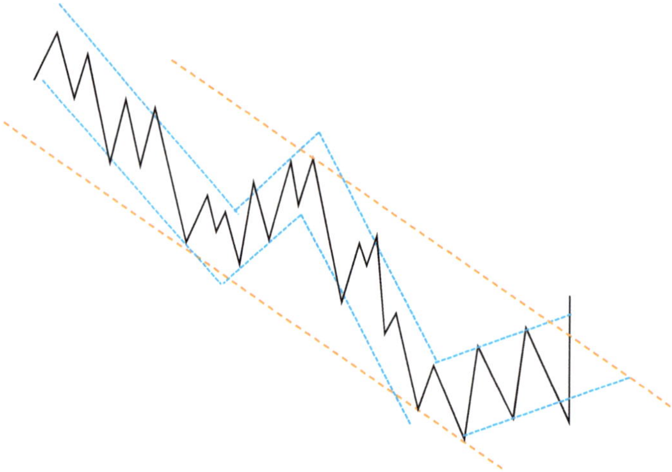

Smaller channels and flags in a wider channel.

IONQ Stock 1min chart: 4 different channels framing the current price movement.

5.4 TARGET PRICES: WHERE DOES THE PRICE TEND TO GO?

Markets have areas which can be considered as magnets or attraction points for the price: meaning there is a high probability that these zones will be retested again. Identifying these zones, allows you

- to properly define your target prices.
- to avoid trades if there is insufficient room for a price movement.

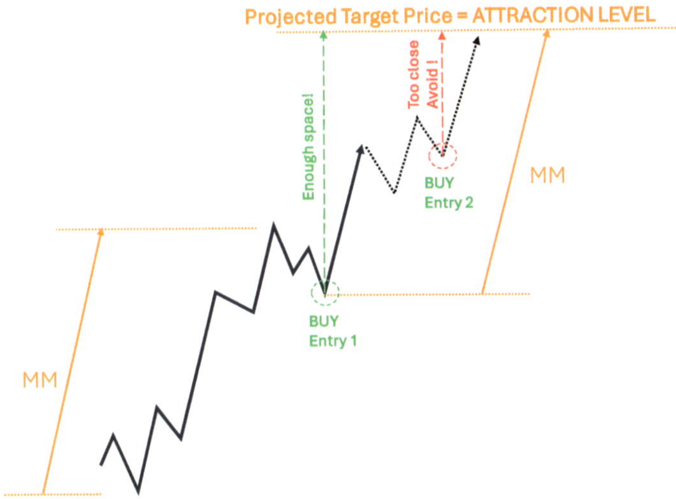

Example of a measured move as strong attraction point. Price touches the measured move and jumps back.

5.4.1 Types of attraction areas

Attraction areas are price zones which are very likely to be retested and can be used as potential target prices. Typical attraction areas are ranges, measured moves, POCs and gaps.

5.4.1.1 Ranges

As explained in Chapter 3.2.1 "Ranges", the middle of the range is an attraction level.

5.4.1.2 Measured moves

Measured moves are also strong attraction areas. In a trending markets price tends to move against measured moves, see Chapter 5.2.

5.4.1.3 POC: Points of Control

The POC represents the price level at which the most trading activity (volume) occurred during a specific period. The POC is a significant magnet because it indicates where the market found the most agreement between buyers and sellers.

See Chapter 4.5.2.4.

5.4.1.4 Gaps

Gaps represent areas where price moved too fast, leaving unfilled orders behind. The market often returns to these levels to fill that missing liquidity.

IMPORTANT: Not all Gaps get filled immediately

while most gaps are retested, the timing varies. Some fill within the same session, while others take days, weeks, or even months.

Example of a gap not being filled immediately.

5.4.2 Retest of a previous swing: a simple and powerfull strategy

One of the most interesting phenomena in trading is the retest of previous swing lows or swing highs, following a strong move in one direction.

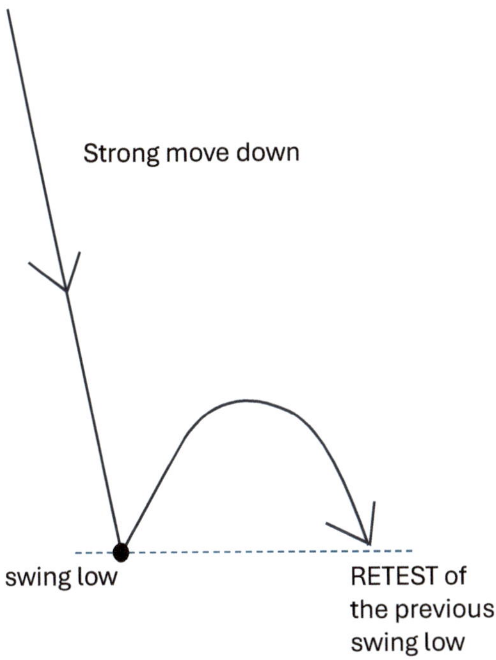

The swing low will be the most probable target price.

This useful and highly probable phenomenon happens in all timeframes, and it is an easy and reliable trading strategy.

Example of a retest of the last swing low. Micron stock 1min chart.

Example of a retest of the previous swing low after a huge run downward. AMD stock 1 min chart.

Example of retest of the previous swing low. NVDA stock.

Example of a retest of the previous swing low, after a very strong movement downward. ES futures contract. 1000 tick chart.

THE RETEST OF THE PREVIOUS SWING AFTER A STRONG MOVEMENT IS A HIGHLY PROFITABLE STRATEGY

5.4.3 Previous day high or low

The highest or lowest swing of the previous day is also considered as a reliable target price for many traders as it is considered a strong support or resistance level and is frequently used to place target prices.

5.4.4 Round numbers

Often, price levels with round numbers (like 1.300, 100.00, etc.) or with significant historical importance are natural support or resistance zones, because using rounding numbers simplifies decision-making, communication, and calculations. That is the reason why professional traders often use them to define entry levels, stop-loss points, take-profit targets.

Micron stock, 1min chart. Price bouncing at exactly 101 $.

6 PRICE ACTION AS A LANGUAGE

A price action trader should become fluent in understanding the nuances and details of price movements. Any chart of a financial instrument is composed of a sequence of candles and patterns, which provide relevant information about who may be in control of the market (if sellers or buyers).

In this chapter, I will explain the most important elements of this language so that you can use them to your advantage.

Price movements can be broken down, like any other language, into smaller, recognizable components:

- Candlestick patterns (the letters).
- Patterns (the words).

I will focus on the most reliable candlesticks and patterns that are really used by professional traders. You will realize that you don't need to know all existing candlestick patterns or every possible geometrical formation to be profitable. Keep it simple and focus on what works.

6.1 CANDLESTICK PATTERNS, THE LETTERS OF THE LANGUAGE

Candlestick patterns are the basic building blocks of price action analysis and are the foundation of price action trading, offering valuable insights into market sentiment, trend direction, and potential reversals.

As you may know a candlestick is a symbol representing a movement of a financial instrument that has occurred within a given time interval. Candlesticks are composed of three elements: a body, wicks and a direction (green=bullish and red=bearish).

A **2-minute candle** represents the price movement of a financial instrument over a **two-minute time interval.**

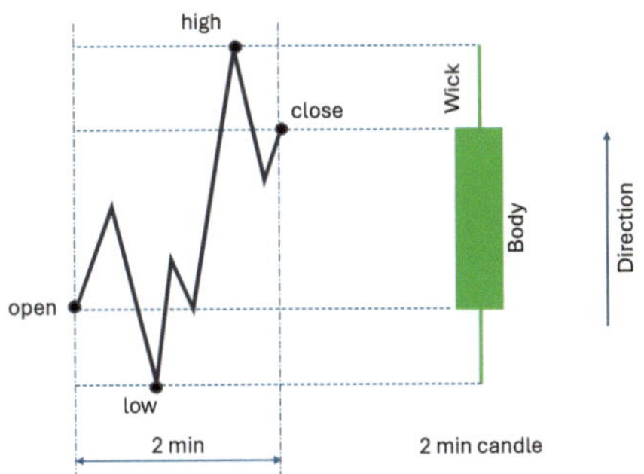

Each candlestick represents a battle between buyers and sellers, and when combined into patterns, they give information about who is in control in the market.

6.1.1 Reliable candlestick patterns as entry signals

There are many candlestick patterns, and countless articles have been written about them. The reality is:

You ONLY need to know 3 candlestick patterns to be a profitable trader

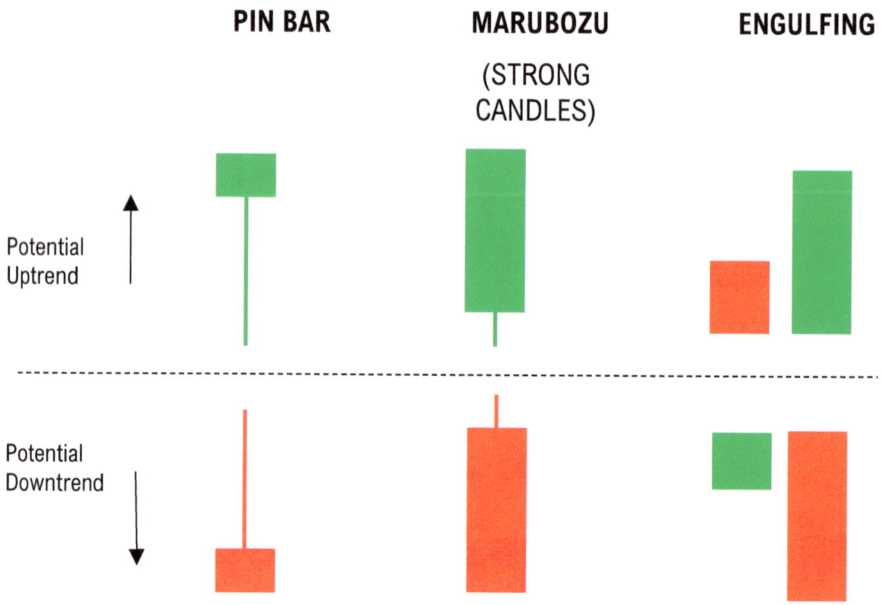

Many retail traders (beginners) think that they need to know all existing patterns. But this is far from the reality. By overcomplicating your trading process, you won't get better results.

You must focus your resources and direct your attention to the highest-quality setups: pin bars, engulfing candles and marubozu candles.

Think of trading like hunting or fishing. A hunter doesn't fire randomly, instead, they wait for the right moment. One well-timed shot is often enough.

> ***KEEP YOUR TRADING AS SIMPLE AS POSSIBLE, ONE GOOD SHOT IS ENOUGH***

According to numerous simulations I have done in C# over the last years, the candlestick patterns mentioned above deliver the best performance when used as entry signals in the right context. See Chapter 7 for detailed guidance on how to trade them.

6.1.1.1 Pin bar (upward move)

Meaning:

- Short-term reversal (down-up).

Geometrical characteristics:

- Body < 0,3 x candle total height.
- The candle total height must be significant related to previous candles.

Risky situations:

- Be cautious with very big pin bar candles, as your stop-loss will need to be set very far away from your entry point, which means you will either need to reduce the size of your trade or use limit orders to enter the trade (see Chapter 10.2. "Limit orders") and still maintain a reasonable risk-reward ratio.

Strong signals (for a long position):

- When the candle closes at or above EMA 21 (exponential moving average of 21 candles) or above a significant support level.
- When the wick begins a few ticks below the previous swing low (see traps in Chapter 6.4.4).

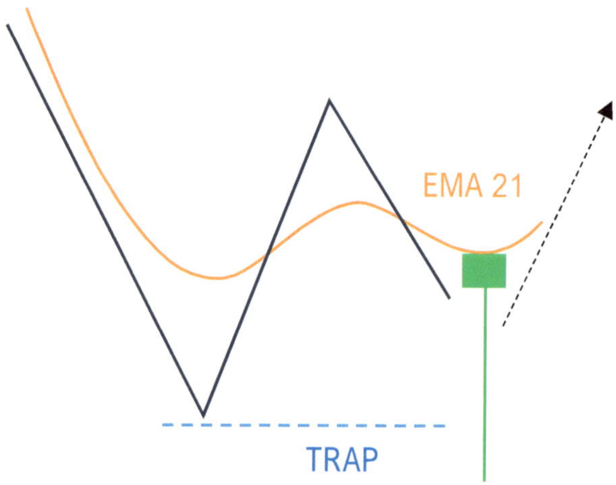

PIN BAR CANDLES ARE THE MOST POWERFUL SIGNAL CANDLES

Example of a red pin bar in a downtrend movement. PLTR stock. 1min chart.

Example of a small green pin bar, not being able to stop the downward movement. ES futures contract. 1000tick chart.

When pin bar candles are too small, meaning their size is too small related to previous candles, they are likely to fail.

6.1.1.2 Engulfing candles (upward move)

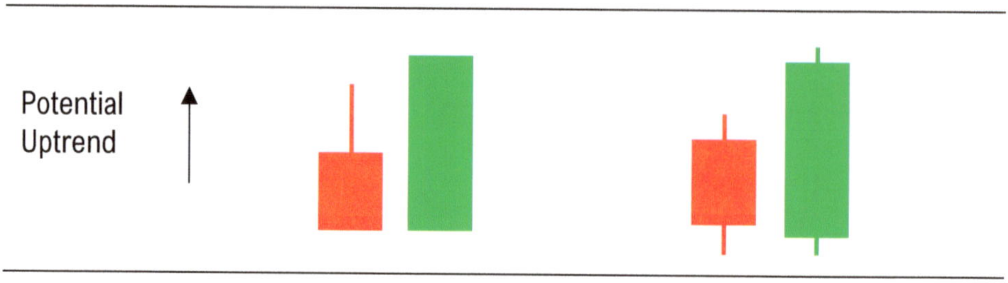

Meaning:

- Short-term reversal (down-up).

Geometrical characteristics:

- The green candle closes above the candle open of the preceding red candle.
- The green candle opens near the close of the previous red candle.
- The total height of the green candle should be significantly larger compared to recent candles.
- Ideally, the green candle closes without a wick on top.

Strong Signals: (for a long trade)

- When engulfing candles are bouncing off EMA 21.
- When the green candle of the engulfing closes at or above EMA 21, without a wick on top.

Engulfing candle bouncing off EMA 21.

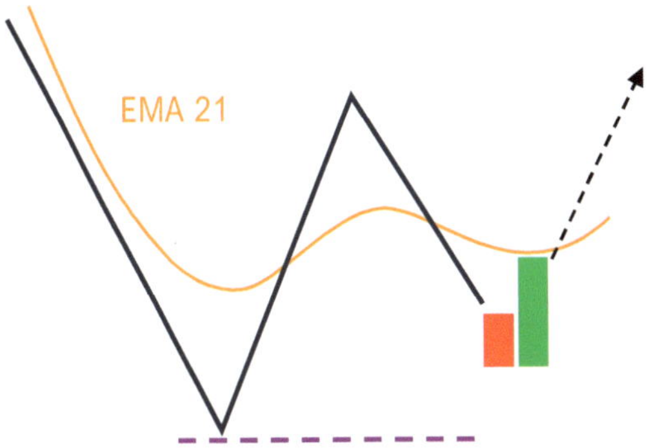

Engulfing candle closing at EMA 21

6.1.1.3 Marubozu (up)

Meaning:

- Marubozu candles are strong candles which usually appear when stop-losses are triggered or when large institutional investors execute substantial trades. Their presence signals strong market momentum.
- Overly large Marubozu candles, might also indicate market exhaustion, suggesting the end of a short-term trend.
- They can serve as confirmation of key support or resistance levels, reinforcing the strength of these levels in the market.

Geometrical characteristics:

- Candle's high = candle's close.
  They should have a small or no wick on top.
- Big body (bigger than previous 14 candles).

Risks:

- When they are too big, use limit orders for an entry, see Chapter 10.1 "Limit orders".

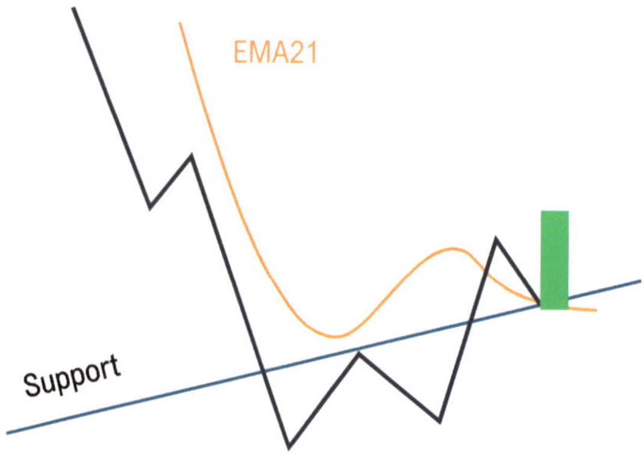

A marubozu *closing strong (without a wick) and jumping off EMA 21.*

Example of several marubozu candles in a downtrend. ES futures contract.

6.1.2 Further candlestick patterns

Most of the candlestick patterns you will find in the literature have no application in trading as they don't have an edge in the market. However, it is important to know the meaning of some of them, as they will provide you with information about the market sentiment.

6.1.2.1 Doji candles

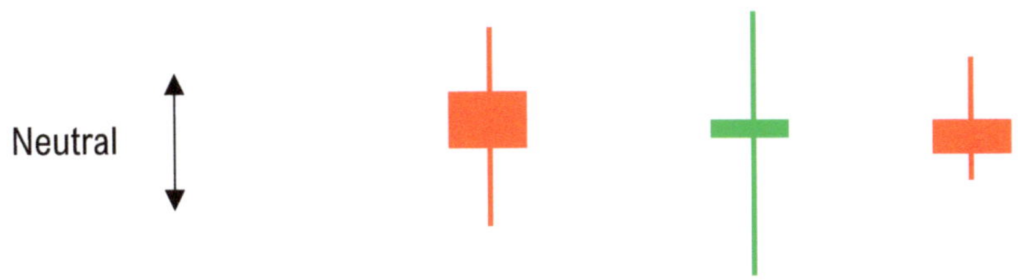

Meaning:

- Indecision in the market.

Geometrical characteristics:

- Small body in the middle.
- Wick above and below the body, with almost the same size.

6.1.2.2 Three soldiers (up)

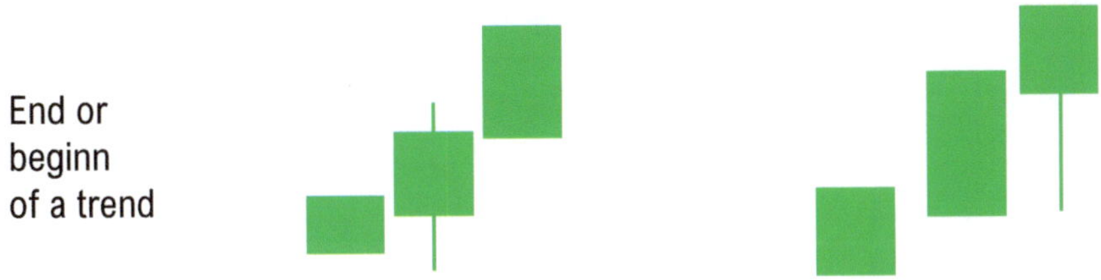

Meaning:

- Strong short-term momentum in one direction (during an uptrend).

Geometrical characteristics:

- Three candles (sometimes 4 candles) moving in the same direction.

Ideal configuration: (for a long trade)

- It is a sign of strong momentum if all three candles are closing strong (without wicks on top).
- When the first candle bounces off a major support or resistance level.

Example of a 3 soldiers pattern. ES futures contract.

6.1.3 Some general rules about candles

The size of the candlestick pattern is a crucial factor in trade validation. While engulfing candles and pin bar candles frequently appear across different areas of the chart, their size, together with their position, plays a significant role in determining the strength of the signal.

6.1.3.1 Candle size

If a candlestick pattern is smaller than the largest candle within the previous 21 candles, it should not be considered a valid entry signal. However, there are exceptions:

For instance, a small green pin bar candle appearing at the end of a strong downward move may present an attractive trading opportunity, as the combination of high reward potential and a tight stop-loss makes the trade worthwhile and could attract many traders.

Example of a small green pin bar, at the end of the movement, after retest of swing low area.

6.1.3.2 Comparing with previous candles

Another valuable approach to understand how markets behave is to analyze how the market has reacted to signal candles and patterns previously. If past occurrences of a pattern did not lead to the expected price movement, it is unlikely that a new occurrence of the same pattern at the same price level will generate a significant reaction.

How did the market react to similar patterns in previous situations?

By consistently comparing candlestick patterns and their corresponding market reactions at different levels, you can develop a better sense of whether a trade is worth the risk.

Strong signal candles in both directions. Contradictory signals. Narrow range.

In the previous example, you can see a series of engulfing candles that might suggest an upward trend. However, the market did not follow through. In fact, there are contradictory signals in both directions.

When you encounter this situation, it's wise to reduce your risk and wait for clearer confirmation. In some cases, switching to a higher timeframe can help filter out misleading entry signals and provide a more reliable market perspective.

Avoid contradictory signals

Even the best candlestick patterns need more ingredients to deliver a good trade. Combine candlestick patterns with momentum, market structure and confluence levels.

In the following chart we see a perfect green pin bar candle failing to revert the price, as the previous overall down movement is too strong and prevails. This is a good example of contradictory signals.

Example of contradictory signals: green pin bar candle after a strong move downward.

In the previous image, the 123 pattern (overall downward movement) shows momentum for the sellers.

The green pin bar candle shows a deceleration of this momentum but it is not strong enough to revert the trend.

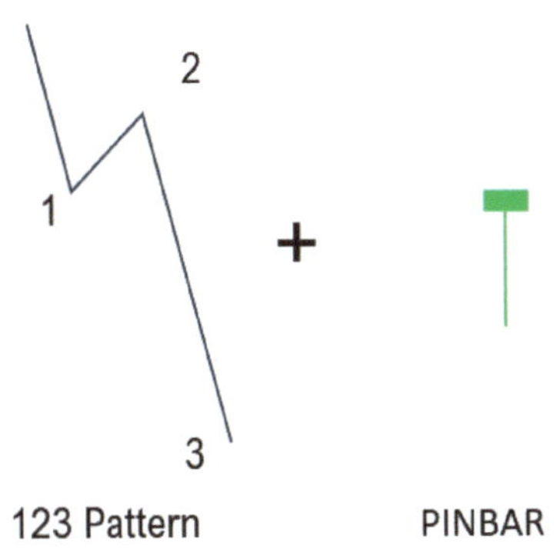

Contradictory signals: 123 down vs. a green pin bar candle.

6.2 ANALYZING PATTERNS

A pattern is a sequence of candlesticks. There are different approaches to analyzing patterns. Let us begin by analyzing the most basic ones, just to give you an idea of what the general analysis process looks like.

Before you start trading, you must understand market behavior. What are typical moves? What do they mean?

Let's start by examining a basic price movement like the following one:

Can you determine the direction in which the market is likely to move if you only see this isolated pattern?

No, patterns like this appear everywhere and can be misleading without additional context.

While many traders might interpret this as a breakout, since price dips below the previous swing low....

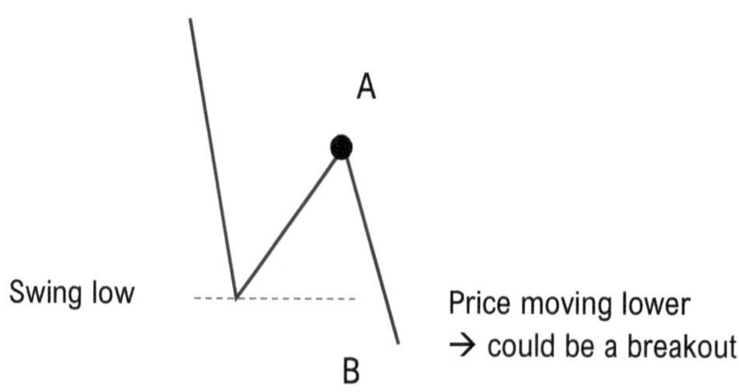

The reality is that price could evolve in several different ways from that point (point B). Here are some common scenarios of how price could move afterward:

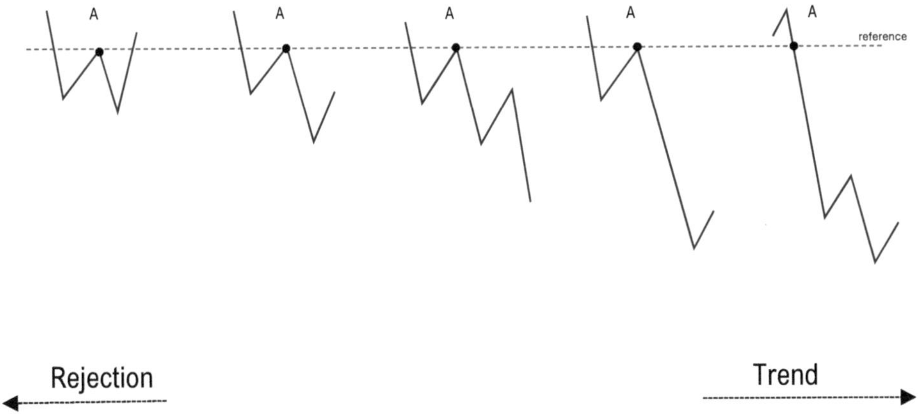

The pattern on the right-hand side shows the strongest momentum compared to the others. From left to right, you can clearly perceive the difference in strength or momentum between each pattern.

This comparison is possible because all patterns share the same reference line (see the line passing through point **A**), which allows you to evaluate their movements relative to this common level.

> ***YOU CAN ONLY COMPARE PATTERNS WHEN THEY SHARE THE SAME REFERENCE LINE (LEVEL)***

The question is, which reference can you use to evaluate price movements,if the market is constantly moving?

6.3 THE IMPORTANCE OF HAVING A REFERENCE: EMA 21

Professional traders use the EMA 21, the "exponential moving average 21".

Price bouncing off the EMA 21 upward. META stock 2min chart.

The price reaction around the EMA 21 can provide valuable insight into the type of market structure you are dealing with:

- Strong directional bounces off the EMA 21 suggest the presence of a **trending market**.

- Price oscillating above and below the EMA 21 indicates a range-bound market. In this case the EMA 21 remains relatively flat and contained within a well-defined price range.

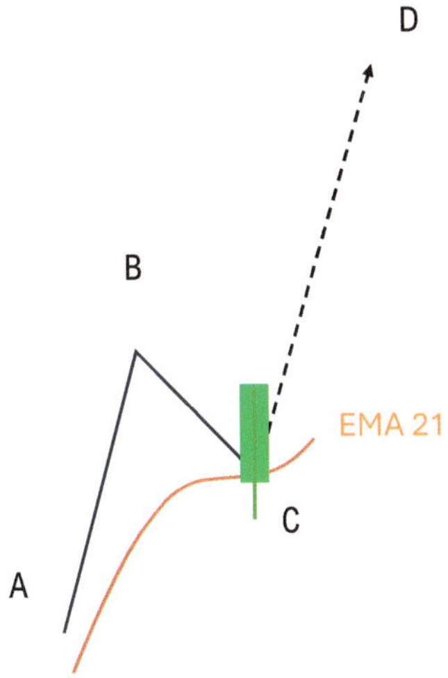

Example of a trending market: price is bouncing off the EMA 21 and the EMA 21 is sloping upward.

Example of a trending market, as price bounces off the EMA 21 downward. AMD stock 1 day chart.

LOOK AT HOW PRICE REACTS TO THE *EMA 21*

Example of a healthy uptrend with the EMA 21 moving upward. Price bouncing off the EMA21. ES futures contract.

Example of a range market, where price oscillates back and forth around the EMA 21. The EMA21 remains nearly flat. IBM stock.

6.4 BASIC PATTERNS: THE WORDS OF PRICE ACTION

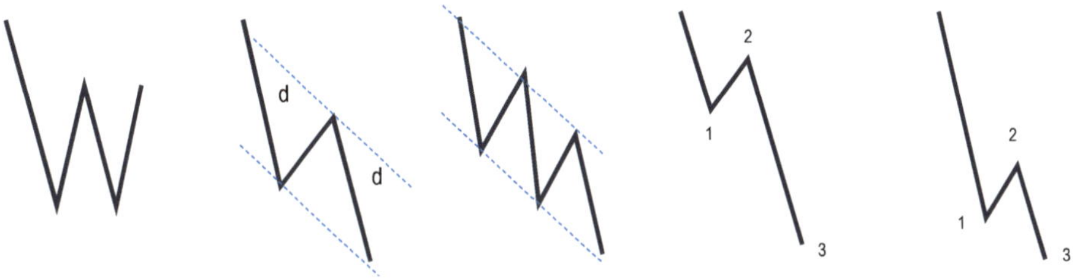

W Pattern | 2-legged retracement | Channel | 123 Pattern | Ray

6.4.1 W AND WV PATTERNS

W and WV signals, also known as double bottom or triple bottom (or double top or triple top depending on the direction) could be reversal signals if spotted in the right context.

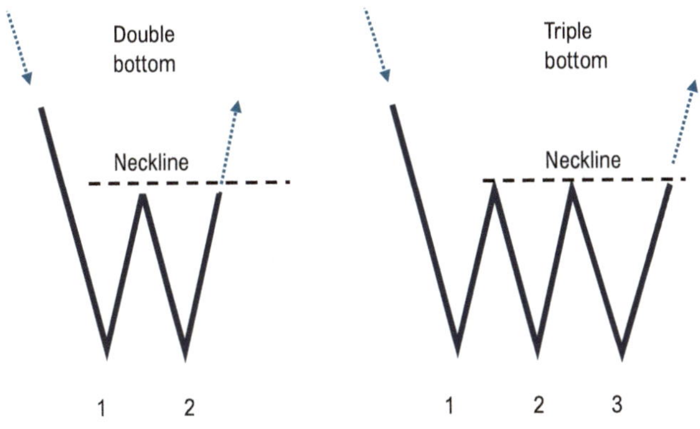

6.4.1.1 Why do W patterns work as reversal patterns?

W signals suggest that asset prices have attempted to move lower twice and failed to break through the previous low. This indicates that selling pressure is weakening and the market may be reaching a point of short-term exhaustion.

The neckline of the double bottom or W pattern is a key point. If the price breaks above this level, it typically triggers further upside movement due to the stop-losses placed by the trapped sellers, providing a solid entry point.

This is the exact explanation of this mechanism:

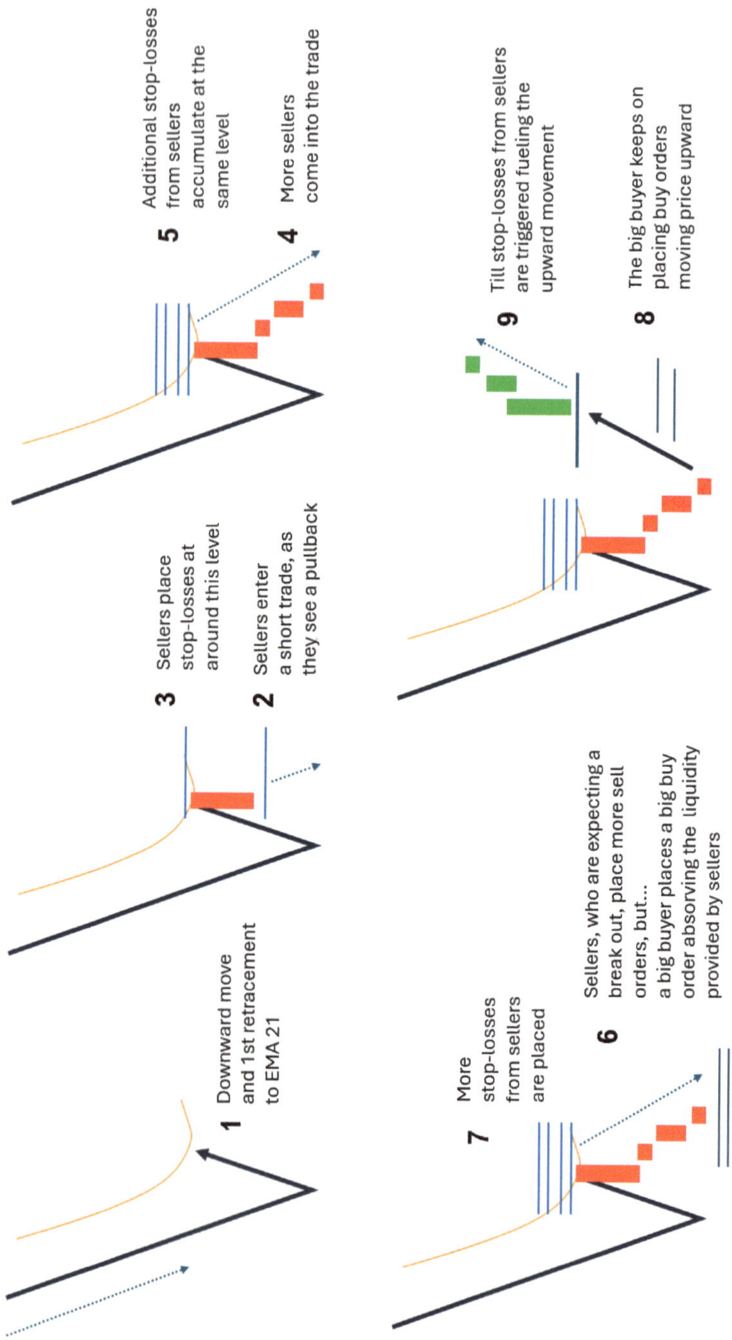

6.4.1.2 *Why do WV patterns work even better?*

The reason why WV patterns do work better, is because sellers try one more time (one more than in W patterns) to push the price lower, which means even more stop-losses (placed by sellers) are going to appear at the neckline of the pattern. If these stop-losses get triggered, the price will move automatically higher, fuelled by them.

Example of W and WV patterns. AMD stock 4 hour chart.

6.4.1.3 *W and VW pattern variations*

W patterns can also look like M patterns when inverted; I will refer to these as inverted W patterns. To simplify the nomenclature, in this book I will mainly refer to the W pattern, regardless of its orientation.

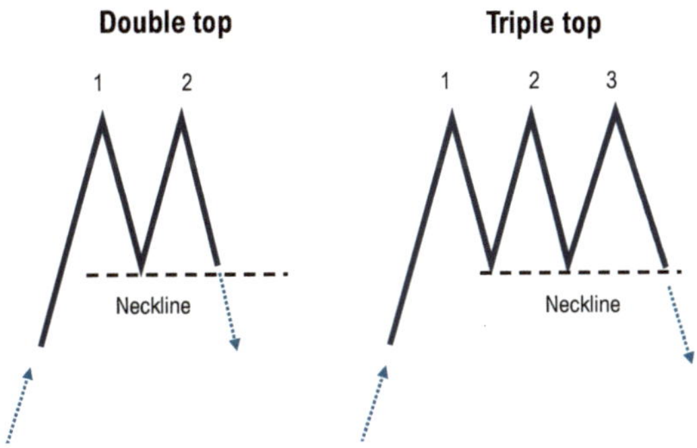

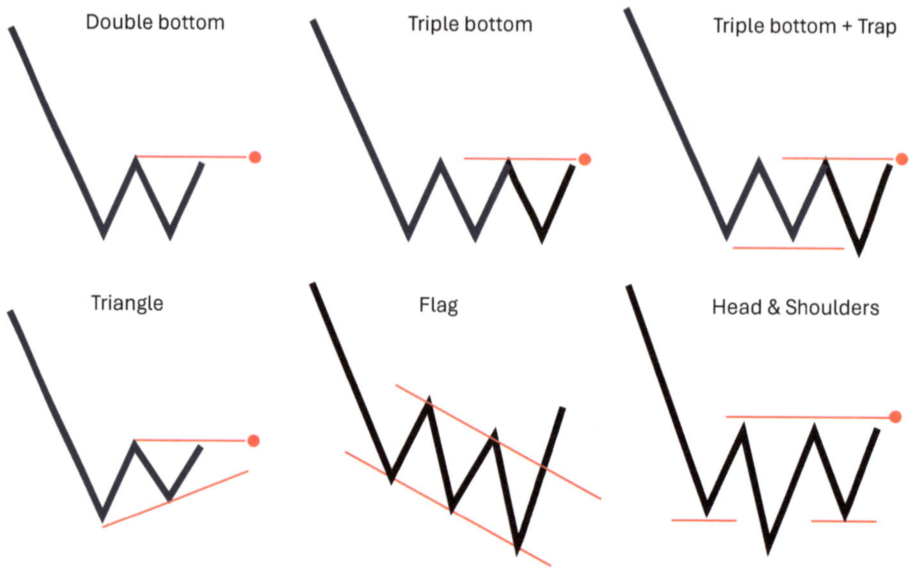

Variations of the W and WV patterns.

Example of W patterns. Micron stock 1 min chart.

6.4.2 Pullbacks

Pullback patterns are one of the most common trend continuation patterns. They are based on strong signal candles bouncing off the EMA 21 and ideally from another support or resistance level. The combination of a previous trend with a strong candle coming from the EMA21 builds the ideal pullback pattern.

They typically appear during strong trends as well as after W patterns. A detailed explanation of how to trade them is provided in Chapter 7.4.

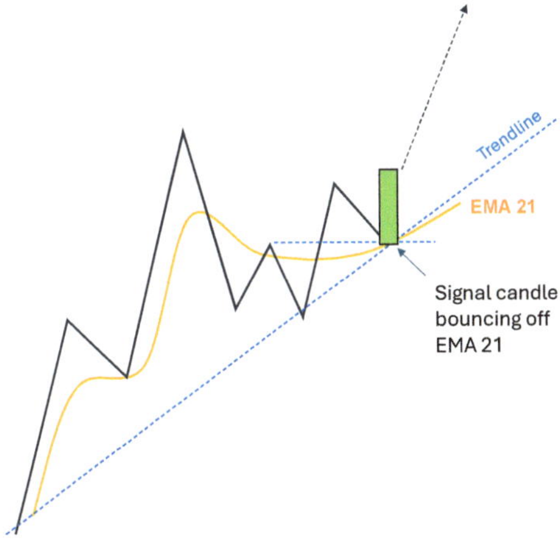

The ideal pullback pattern, appearing after a W pattern.

Example of a pullback pattern. See the signal candle (red pin bar candle) bouncing off the EMA21 in a downtrend, after a strong momentum downward.

6.4.3 123 Patterns

123 patterns are easy to detect, and they can appear in many different timeframes.

They are composed of 3 parts: one leg, a retracement leg in the opposite direction and a second leg.

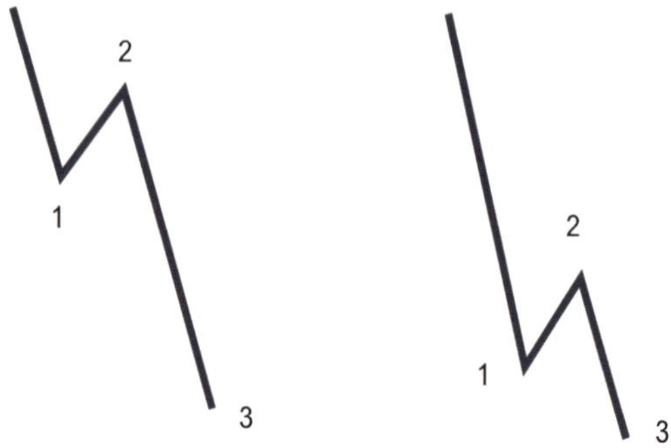

Depending on the size of their legs and on the location where they appear, they can have different meanings. They may signal the **beginning of a trend,** or simply represent **a two-legged retracement.**

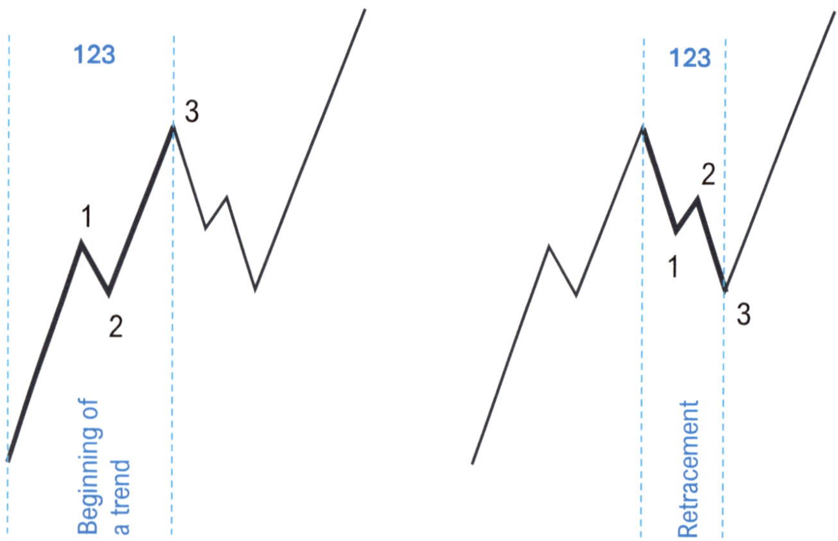

Difference between the beginning of a trend and a retracement.

6.4.3.1 123 movement: the beginning of a trend

A 123 pattern, which usually means the beginning of a trend, looks as follows:

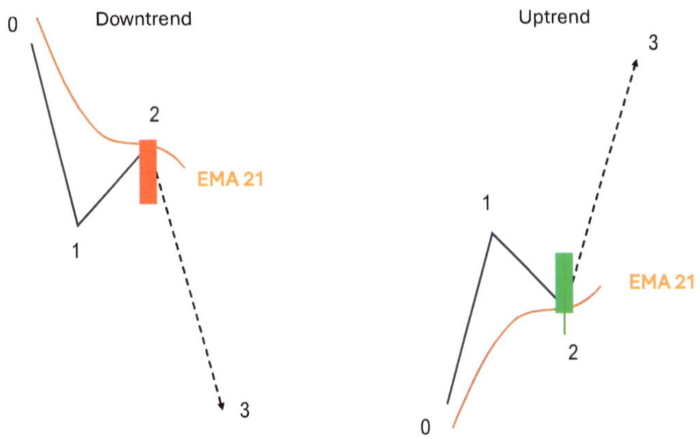

Conditions:

- Leg 2-3 is larger than leg 0-1.
- Leg 2-3 starts at or around EMA 21 and shows a clear push in the direction of the main move.

> ***IF THE SECOND LEG OF A 123 PATTERN IS BIGGER THAN THE FIRST ONE, AND THE SECOND LEG STARTS AT OR AROUND THE EMA 21, THE BEGINNING OF A TREND IS VERY PROBABLE***

6.4.3.2 123 movement as a Retracement

A retracement is a short-term price movement against the main trend and does not indicate the beginning of a new trend.

Retracements can have 1, 2 or 3 legs and can be embedded in small channels.

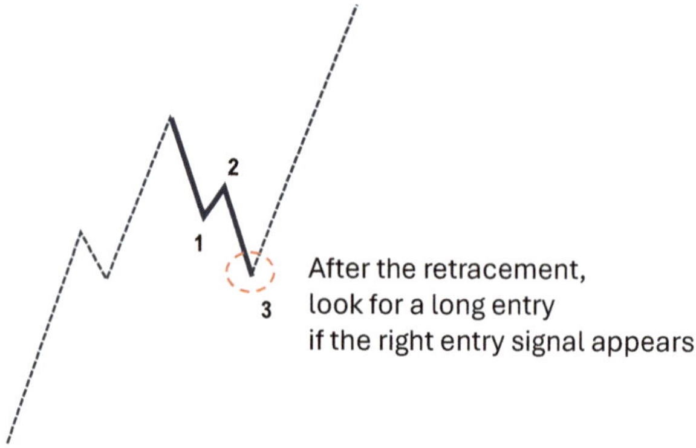

The advantage of retracements is that they provide the possibility to buy low. Professional traders will be looking for an entry signal around Point 3.

USE RETRACEMENTS TO ENTER AN EXISTING TREND AT A BETTER PRICE

Example of a 2-legged retracement and trendline coming down after a 123 movement upward.

6.4.4 Trap: The Failing Breakout

Breakouts occur when price moves decisively beyond a key level of support or resistance, often signaling strong momentum. Successful breakouts are typically accompanied by high volume, which often helps confirm the validity of the move.

Traps are failed breakouts. They occur when price breaks above a resistance level, or another key technical level, leading traders to believe a breakout is happening. Shortly afterward, price reverses sharply downward, trapping buyers who entered long positions.

In a **bear trap**, price falls below a key level, tempting sellers to enter short positions. Price then reverses higher, forcing them to exit, see the difference between a trap and a breakout in the following image.

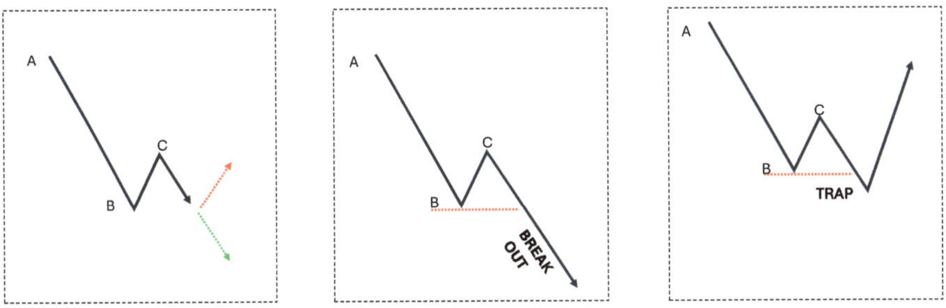

In a **bull trap**, price moves above a key level, attracting buyers, but then quickly drops, hitting their stop-losses.

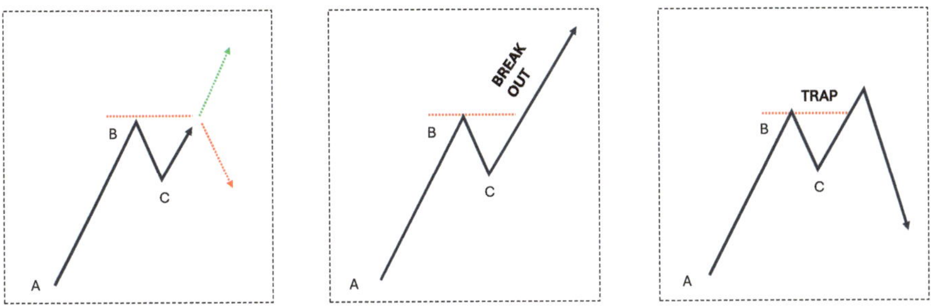

Traps often occur in areas of high liquidity, where traders caught on the wrong side are forced to exit at a loss. Institutional investors anticipate these price levels and use them as opportunities to place large orders against the prevailing retail sentiment, allowing them to take advantage of the liquidity.

A trap combined with a major support or resistance level and a pin bar candle may be a very reliable trade.

Example of trap patterns in an uptrend. ES futures contract. 1000 tick chart.

A trap pattern and an engulfing pattern as short-term reversal signal in 1h chart. AMD stock.

6.4.5 THE MOMENTUM PATTERN

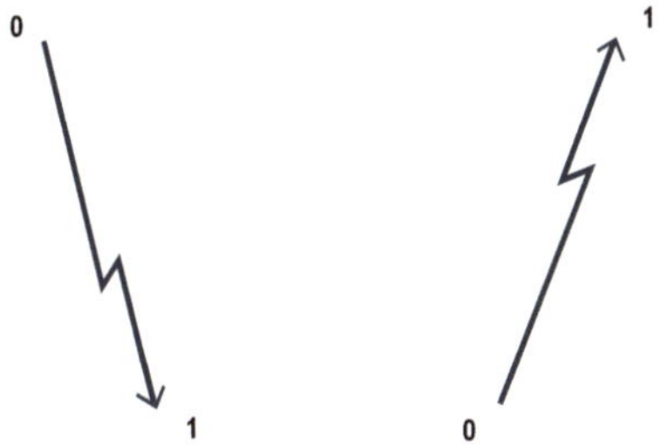

The **momentum** pattern usually happens after a pullback or after a trap pattern. They are based on a strong straight move in the direction of the trend and are usually composed of 4 to 6 (not more) strong candles moving in the same direction.

Example of bullish "momentum patterns", composed of 4 and 6 candles.

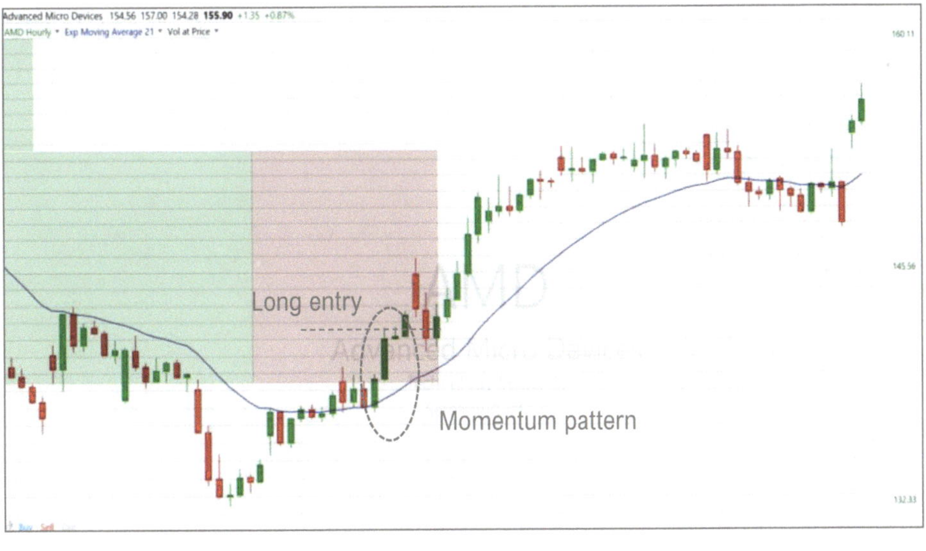

Example of a bullish momentum pattern, 1h chart, AMD stock.

How can you trade the momentum pattern in an uptrend?

Just go long the close of the next red candle and set your stop-loss below the EMA21. Go for RR = 1 for the first target price, meaning your risk is not greater than your potential reward. The concept of RR will be explained in Chapter 9.1.

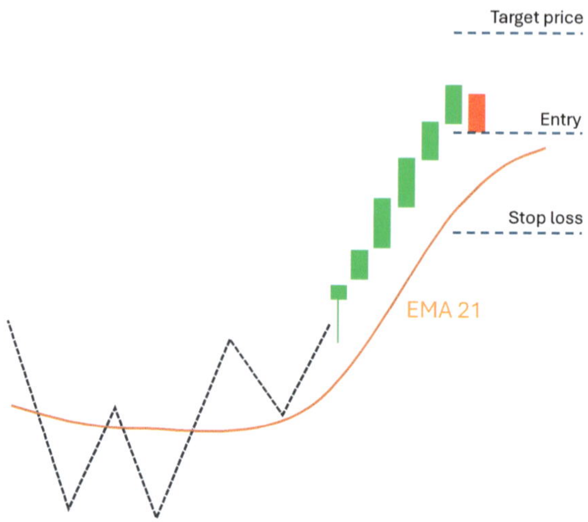

6.5 IDEAL PRICE ACTION SEQUENCES

When markets have a clear direction, you can recognize it, because a sequence of patterns appears. One of the most common movements is the following one:

6.5.1 THE MOST COMMON PRICE ACTION SEQUENCE

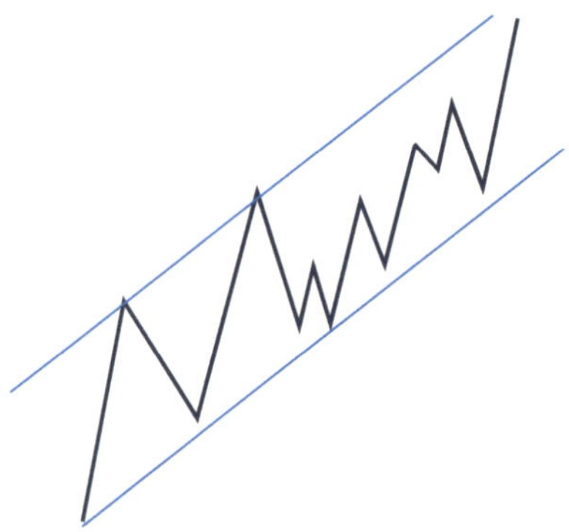

Which patterns can you recognize in this price movement?

Let us put all pieces together, we have learned so far.

This market movement is composed of the following elements:

1. 123 pattern.
2. Retracement.
3. W pattern.
4. Pullback pattern.
5. Trap pattern.
6. Momentum pattern.

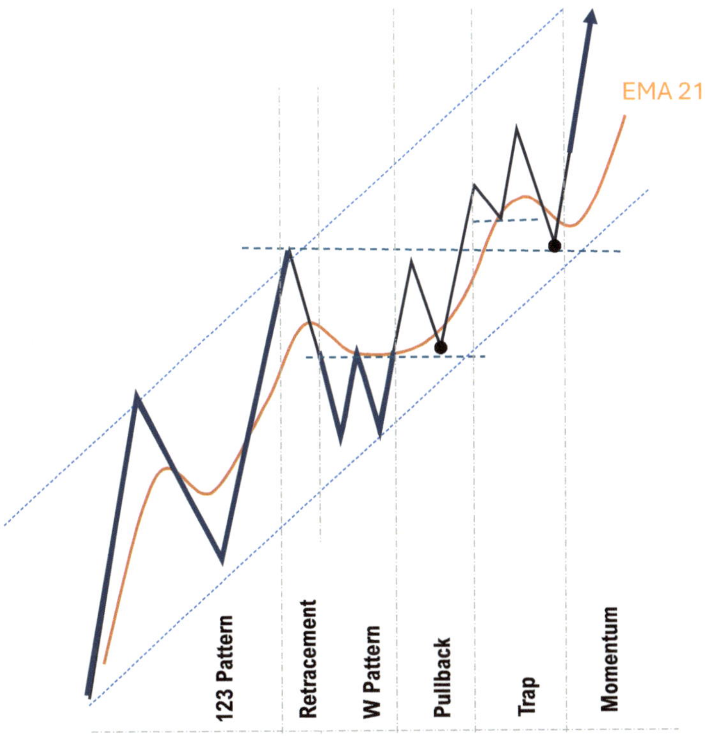

Ideal price action sequence

This sequence normally shows up, when there is a healthy trend.

REMEMBER THIS PRICE ACTION SEQUENCE !

Example of a price action cycle: W + Pullback + Momentum. ES futures contract. 1000 tick chart.

This sequence of patterns occurs across many liquid markets.

THE BEST-LOOKING EXAMPLES ARE OFTEN FOUND IN THE FUTURES MARKET, PARTICULARLY THE NQ (NASDAQ) AND ES (S&P 500), WHEN USING TICK CHARTS

While the ideal price action sequence can also appear on time-based charts, it tends to occur less frequently and with less clarity than in tick charts.

6.5.2 THE PRICE ACTION SEQUENCE WITH A TRAP SETUP

There is another important price action sequence which contains a trap pattern and looks like this:

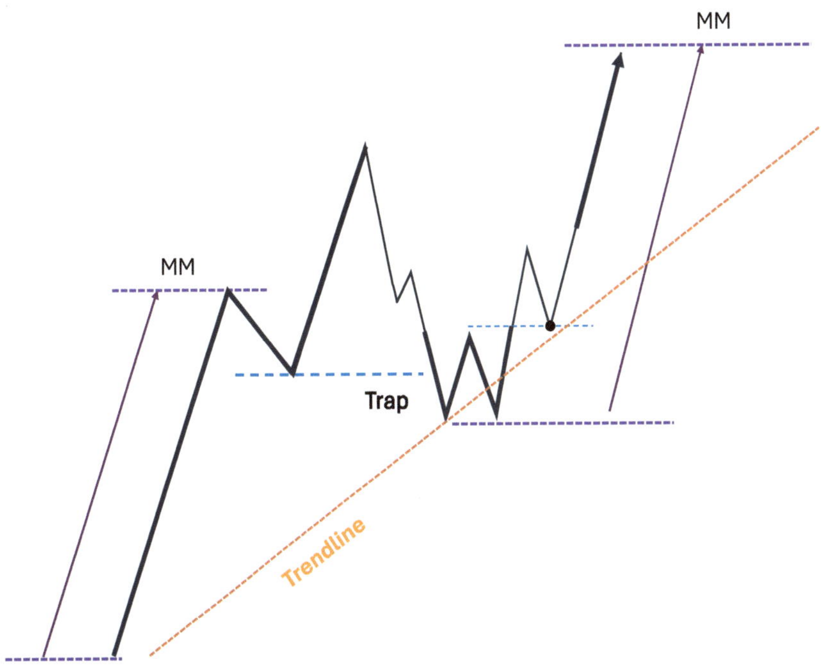

Price action sequence with a trap pattern in an uptrend.

These are the elements you can recognize in this example, see image above:

1. 123 Pattern.
2. Retracement.
3. W Signal at trap level.
4. Pullback Signal.
5. Momentum Pattern.

How to trade this sequence in detail will be explained in Chapter 7.

Example of a price cycle sequence with a trap setup. ES futures contract.

Example of a price cycle sequence with a trap setup. In this case the trap signal is a W pattern at the same time.

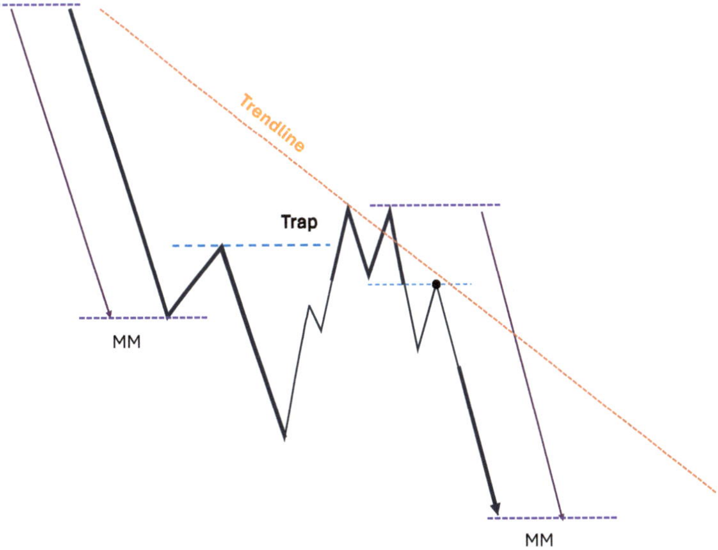

Price action sequence with a trap pattern in a downtrend.

Example of a price action sequence downward with a trap pattern and measured moves. Tesla Stock 1 min chart.

7 ADVANCED PATTERNS: HOW TO TRADE THEM IN DETAIL

7.1 TRADING THE IDEAL PRICE CYCLE SEQUENCE WITH A TRAP PATTERN

Why does this price action cycle work?

If you look at the different components of the price action cycle, you will realize that all of them make sense:

- **The 123 pattern** is telling you that a trend has begun.
- The **retracement** allows you to buy at a better price.
- The **W pattern** fuels your trade due to the stop-losses of your opponents.
- The **channel** gives you the reference of what is a high or a low price.
- Both the **retest of the trendline** formed during the retracement movement and the **trap level** confirm that this is an ideal entry point, as there is strong confluence at this level.

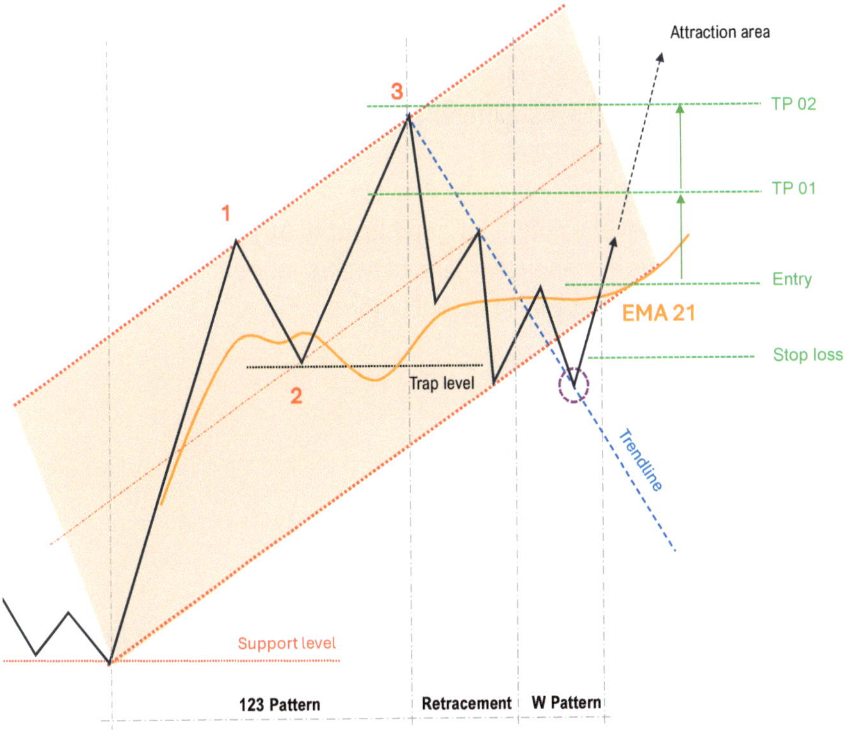

How to trade the ideal price cycle sequence with a trap pattern:

- Look for a 123 pattern and a retracement.
- After that, as soon as price crosses down the EMA 21, look for a W pattern or a strong candle closing at the EMA 21.
- The entry point is at the EMA 21 or at the necklace of the W pattern.
- You can use 2 target prices (TPs). The first one (TP 01) at RR=1 (Risk = Reward) and second one (TP 02) at the previous swing high of the overall move.

...AND REGARDLESS OF THE STRATEGY YOU USE, DON'T FORGET THE BASIC RULES FOR a GOOD TRADE:

- **Look for attraction points** to confirm your trade direction is right.

- **Define a realistic target price by identifying key support and resistance levels,** as discussed in Chapter 5.4.

  To maximize profit potential, it is recommended to define two or three different target prices at different price levels, depending on the strength of the uptrend movement.

- **Which price level would be a good level to buy?**
  Make sure there is enough space between your entry point and the next support or resistance level to justify the trade.

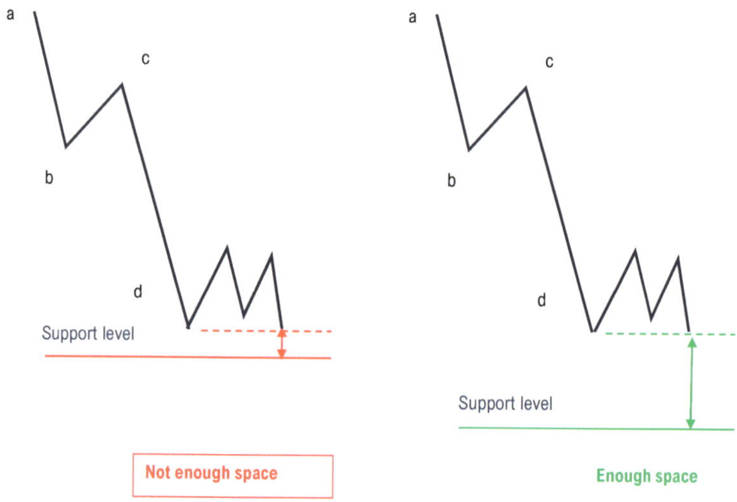

When point D is very close to a support level (such as a trendline or a horizontal support/resistance level), the price does not have enough room to move. This means the potential reward is too small to justify the risk of entering a trade at that level.

If price is too high after the 123 movement, wait for a retracement (a corrective move in the opposite direction of the trend). A good area to start looking for an entry signal is after price crosses below the 21 EMA.

- **Why do we wait for a retracement?**
  Markets move in waves and often forming channels or other types of patterns (see Chapter 5.3). The best time to enter a trade is typically when a retracement aligns with a retest of the lower boundary of a

pattern or channel. To identify this, draw a channel as explained in Chapter 4.2.

- **Buy low sell high:**
  Once you've defined your target prices, the next step is to identify a suitable entry point. The logic is the same as in real life: if you know the price at which you can sell an asset (your target), it becomes easier to determine the price at which it's worth buying (your entry level).

  Analyze how price has behaved in the past. Use historical data to identify what can be considered a "high" or a "low" price within the current market context.

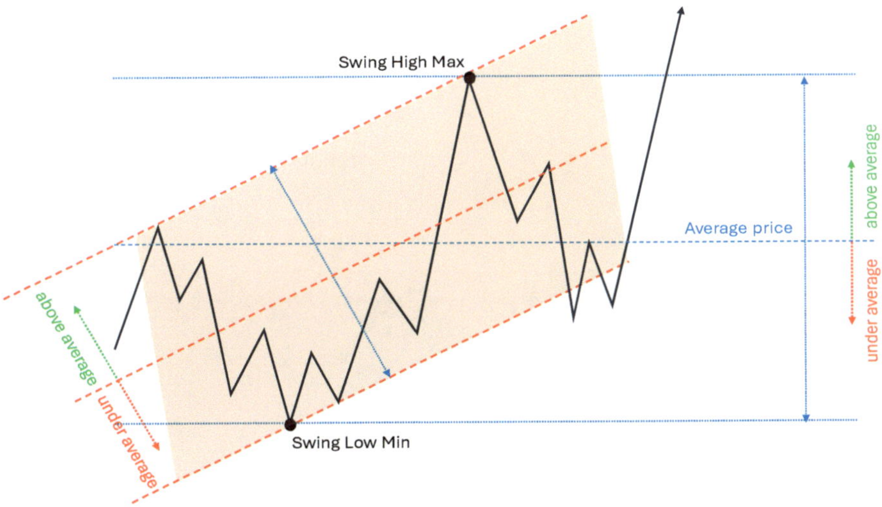

- **Look for a Trap level**
  Trap levels are often key levels of support or resistance.

- **Look for areas where stop-losses are likely to accumulate.**
  Identify levels where opposing traders may have placed their stop-loss orders. Once triggered, these levels can fuel your trade by creating momentum in your favor.

By being patient and waiting for the right entry area, where all these ingredients align, you reduce the risk and increase potential reward. This is exactly what professional traders and algorithms consistently aim to achieve.

7.1.1 How to trade a W pattern after a 2-legged retracement?

Retracements usually have one or two legs. When a **retracement** is **made of two legs**, an additional important factor to consider is the trendline formed by these two legs. This trendline often represents a relevant resistance level, meaning no trade should be executed below it.

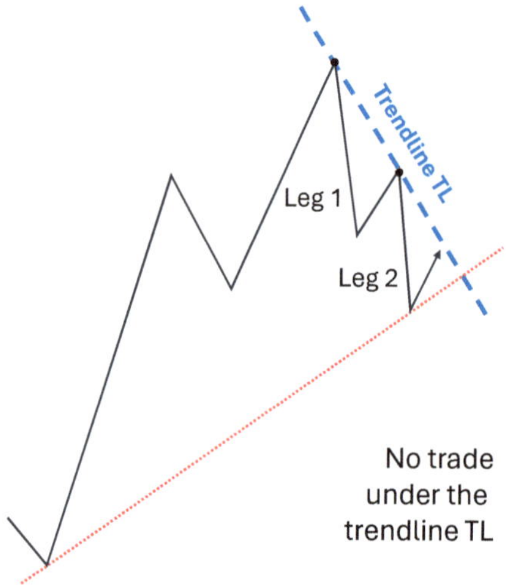

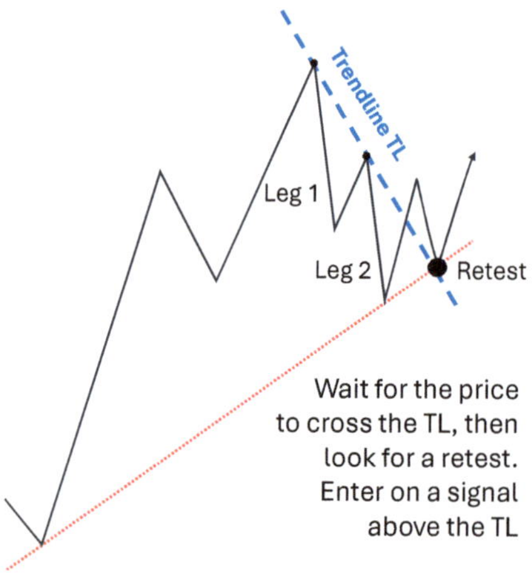

Any entry below the trendline is too risky. Therefore, wait for price to clearly break above the trendline and then retest it. A long trade should only be considered if price bounces off the trendline (see image above) and forms a strong signal candle. If the signal candle closes strongly (with little to no upper wick) and ends near the EMA 21, the trade can be taken with confidence, as this represents a high-probability setup.

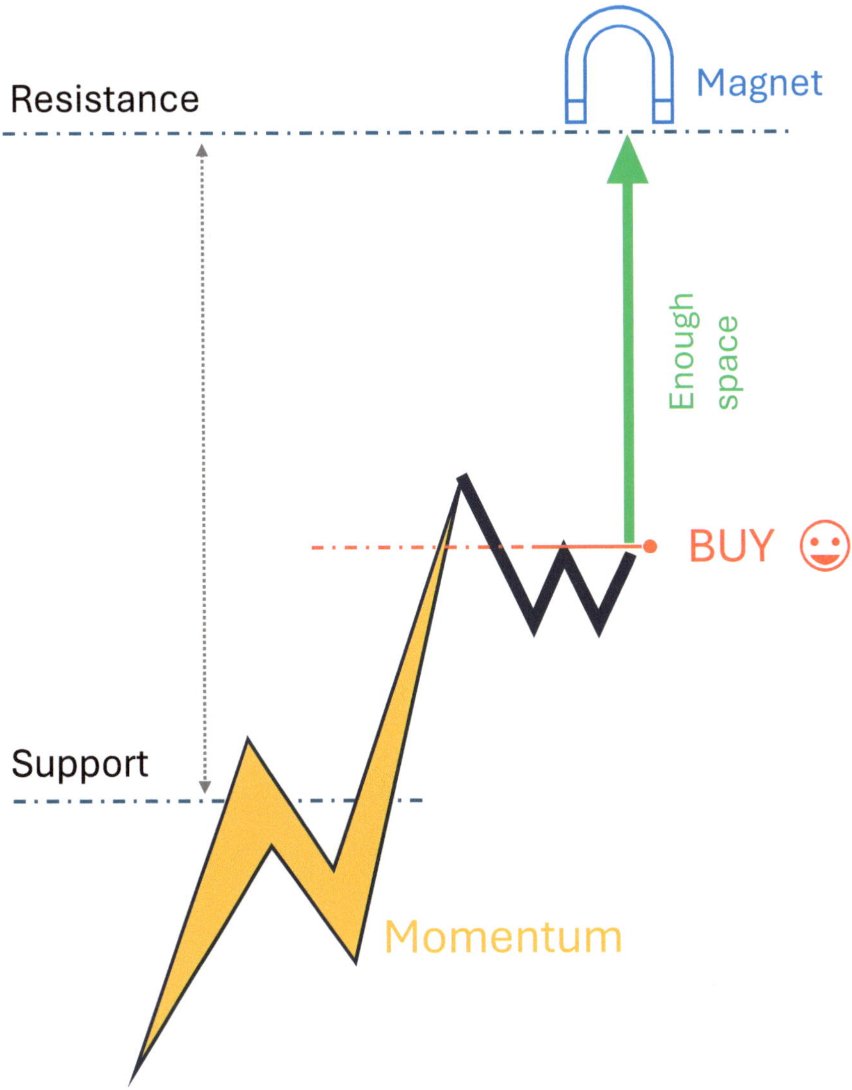

General recipe for a good trade.

Main components of a good trade:

- Support level
- Momentum
- Entry signal and pattern
- Magnet
- Enough space (good Risk-Reward-Ratio)

CHECKLIST: TRADING A W PATTERN AFTER A 2 - LEGGED RETRACEMENT

1. MOMENTUM IN ONE DIRECTION STARTED AT THE 123- PATTERN, NOW WE KNOW, THAT MOMENTUM IS ON OUR SIDE. AND WE CAN DRAW THE CHANNEL (SEE CHAPTER 4.2.2).
2. WE WAIT FOR A RETRACEMENT (PRICE CROSSING EMMA 21), LOOKING TO FIND A BETTER ENTRY POINT AT THE LOWEST PART OF THE CHANNEL.
3. WAIT FOR A RETEST OF THE BOTTOM LINE OF THE CHANNEL.
4. LOOK FOR A W PATTERN AT SUPPORT LEVEL, WHERE YOU FIND MULTIPLE CONFLUENCE. THE NECKLINE OF THE W PATTERN SHOULD BE AT AROUND EMA 21.
5. WE ALSO KNOW WHERE THE PRICE SHOULD GO AND WHICH LEVELS ARE GOOD AND RELIABLE AS TARGET PRICES.
   DEFINE A RELIABLE TARGET PRICE ACCORDING TO THE AVAILABLE ATTRACTION POINTS.
6. ONLY ENTER A TRADE IF THERE IS NO TREND LINE OBSTRUCTING YOUR MOVE UPWARD.
7. ONLY ENTER THE TRADE IF THERE IS ENOUGH SPACE BETWEEN YOUR ENTRY AND THE PREVIOUSLY DEFINED TARGET: THE RISK-REWARD SHOULD BE GREATER THAN ONE.
8. ONCE YOU HAVE ENTERED THE W TRADE, MAKE SURE TO DEFINE THE PROPER STOP-LOSS ACCORDING TO THE EXISTING VOLATILITY. SEE CHAPTER 9.4.
9. SET TWO OR THREE TARGET PRICES. THE FIRST TARGET PRICE ACCORDING TO RR = 1. THE SECOND TARGET PRICE AT THE FIRST RESISTANCE LEVEL AND THE 3RD TARGET PRICE AT THE TOP LINE OF THE CHANNEL OR AT THE MEASURED MOVE.
10. ONCE YOUR FIRST TARGET PRICE IS ACHIEVED, MOVE YOUR STOP-LOSS TO BREAK EVEN, WHICH IS THE ENTRY LEVEL OF YOUR TRADE.
11. IF PRICE KEEPS ON MOVING UPWARD FROM TARGET PRICE 1, MAKE SURE YOUR WINNING TRADE IS PROTECTED BY TRAILING YOU STOP AND LOCKING IN PROFITS (SEE CHAPTER 9.5)

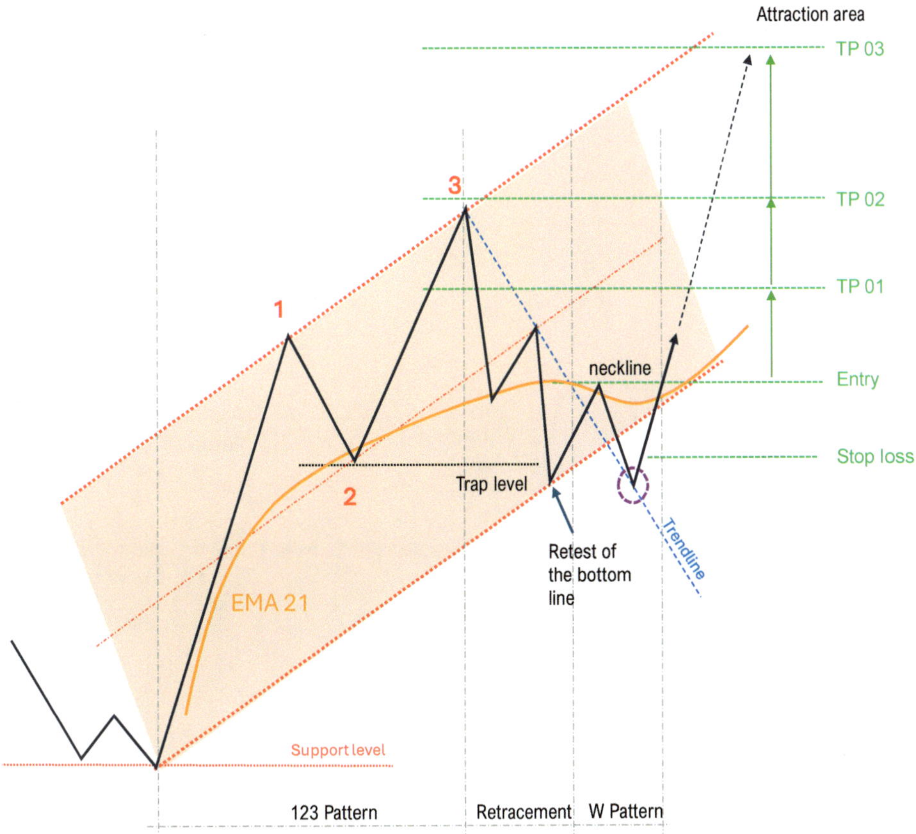

Trading a W pattern after a 2-legged retracement.

7.1.2 Additional trade entry signals after a W pattern

After an entry signal like a W pattern, you still might find the following trading opportunities and entry signals depending on the strength of the movement. These are the typical patterns following a W pattern.

1. **A pullback**: when price bounces off EMA 21. See Chapter 6.4.2.
2. **A momentum trade**: they appear after W patterns or pullback patterns. See Chapter 6.4.5.

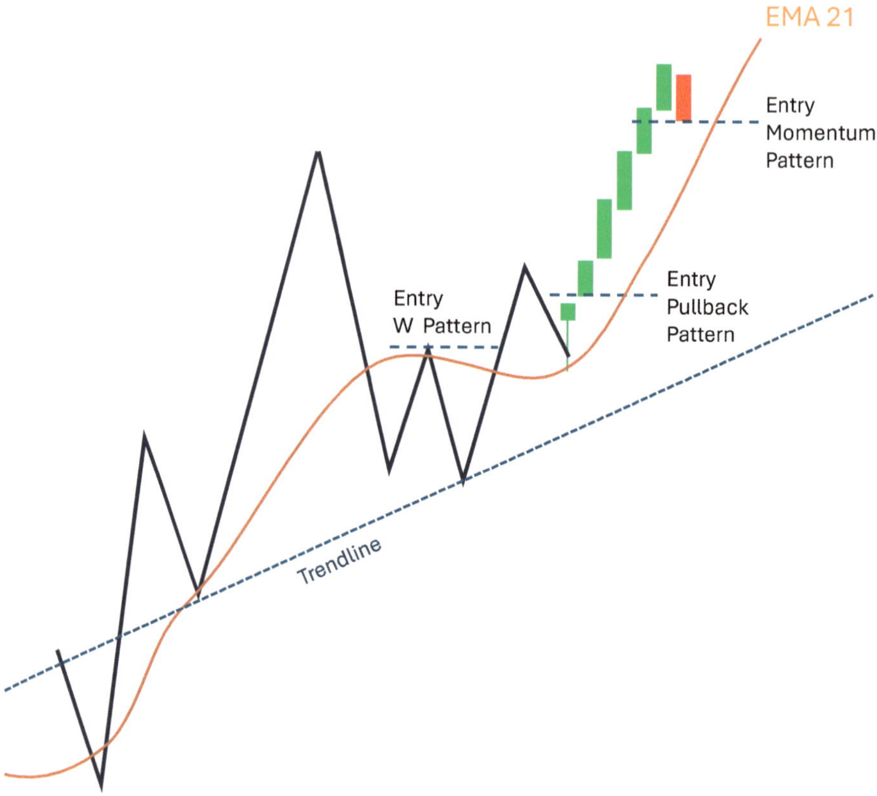

Sequence of trades: a W pattern, a pullback pattern and a momentum pattern.

7.2 TRADING RANGES LIKE A PRO

7.2.1 IDENTIFYING RANGES

When a range appears, it must be obvious. There must be a repetition of bounces at the same price levels in both directions.

7.2.2 FUNDAMENTAL CHARACTERISTICS

As we saw in Chapter 3.2.1.1 **ranges act as a magnet**. You can expect price to be attracted by the range at some point. Therefore, professional traders use ranges as target prices.

When professional traders approach ranges, they look at the following zones for buying and selling.

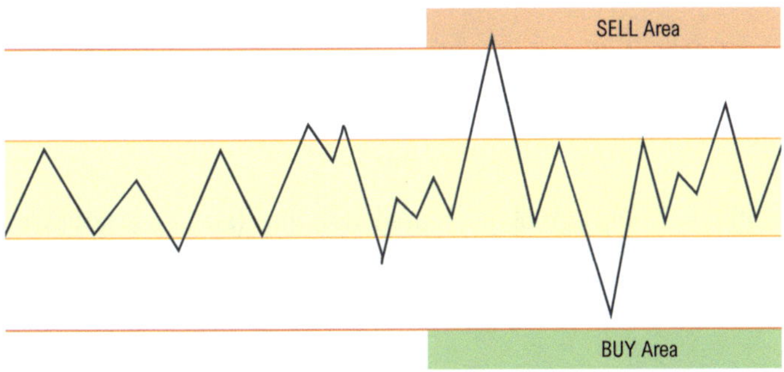

Favorite zones for professional buyers and sellers in a range bound market.

The direction of the price inside the range can be very random and unpredictable:

DON'T TRADE INSIDE THE RANGE

7.2.3 How to trade ranges

1. Once you have recognized the range take the width of the range and draw 2 parallel lines to it, they are called **deviation lines**, like this:

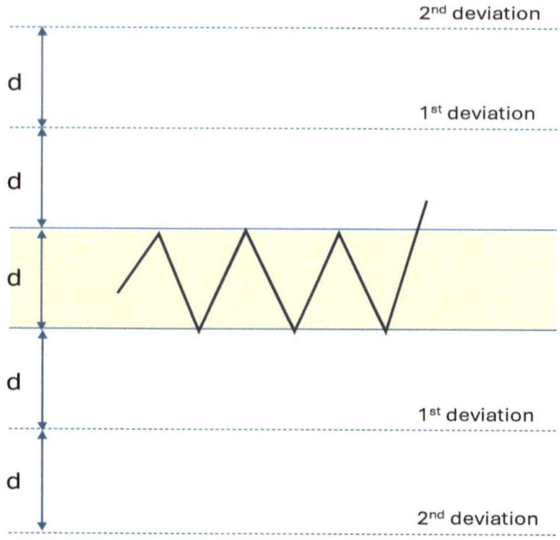

2. Look for an entry signal at these defined deviations lines, as **they act as support and resistance** levels.

Example 1: Entry signal at 1st deviation line (see inverted W pattern)

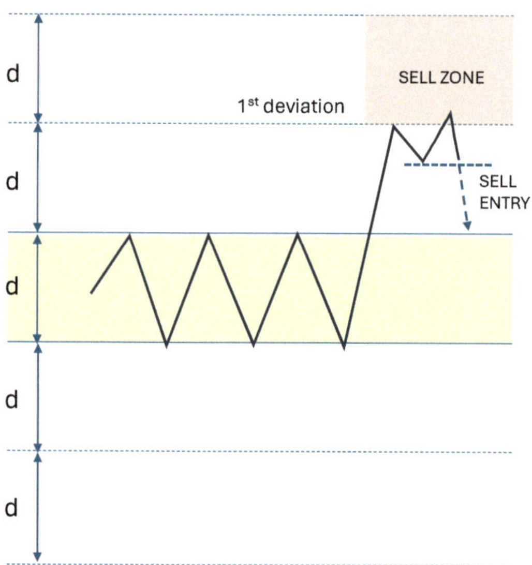

A W pattern is appearing at the 1st deviation line of a range.

Example 2: Entry signal at 2nd deviation line

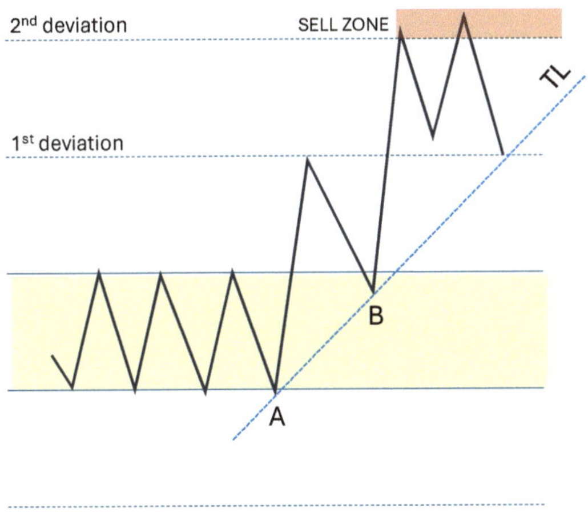

W Signal appearing at the 2nd deviation line of a range.

In this case, the trendline (TL) defined by A and B is an obstacle on the way down. You will need to wait for the price to cross the trendline.

The right entry signal will be a pullback bouncing off the trendline like this:

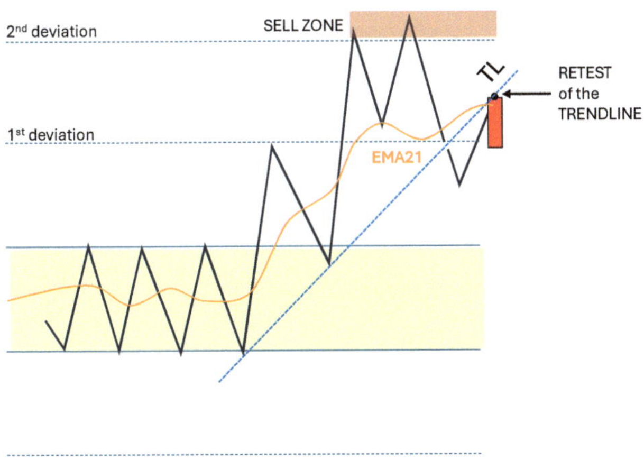

3. Conditions to enter a short position in a range:
   a. **Price moves downward**, crossing below the EMA 21 and the trendline.
   b. **A retracement** back toward the trendline.
   c. **A retest of the trendline**, meaning price must touch (retest) the trendline.
   d. **A strong rejection candle** bouncing off the trendline.

7.2.4 PROBABLE TARGET PRICES IN A RANGE

Your target prices should be placed at the different deviation lines, as shown below:

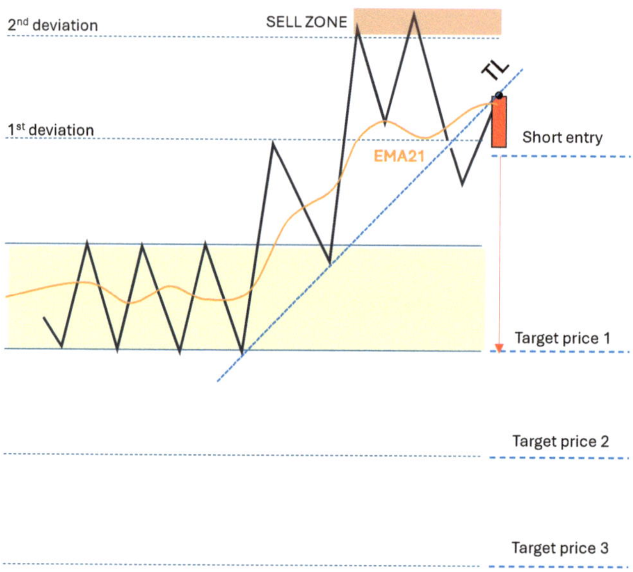

DEVIATION LINES IN RANGES ACT AS SUPPORT AND RESISTANCE LEVELS

Example of a real trade in a range at 1st deviation. Meta stock, 2 min chart.

Example of a range and entry signal at a strong red candle. ES futures contract.

As you can see, ranges in the stock market, do not always form clear or easily recognizable patterns. To trade them effectively, you must apply a certain level of abstraction and accept a certain degree of imperfection. However, In the futures market ranges use to be cleaner and easier to recognize.

7.2.5 Does a range always act as an attraction area?

There is one case, in which the range might not act as a magnet anymore, at least in the short term.

If you see the price bouncing strong off the EMA 21, it means a new uptrend has started (see 123 patterns in Chapter 6.4.3). You will also see that the 2nd deviation is being clearly crossed.

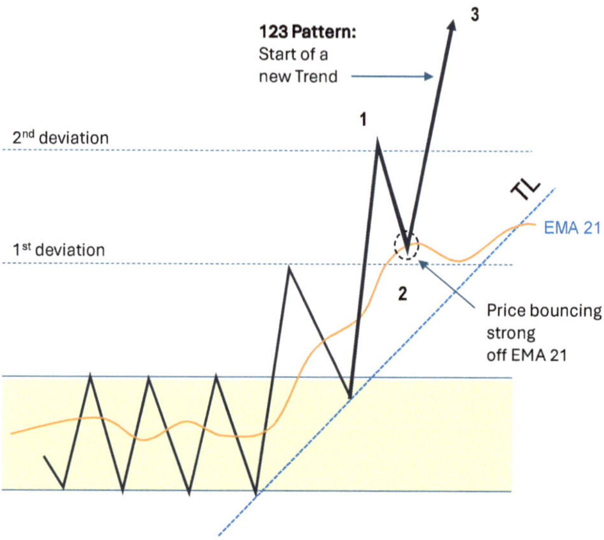

Example of a 123 pattern after a range.

7.3 TRIANGLES

Triangles behave like ranges. The middle of the triangle is not a good area to trade, as there is usually not enough space for a significant price movement. However, the midpoint can be used as an attraction area and, therefore, as a target price.

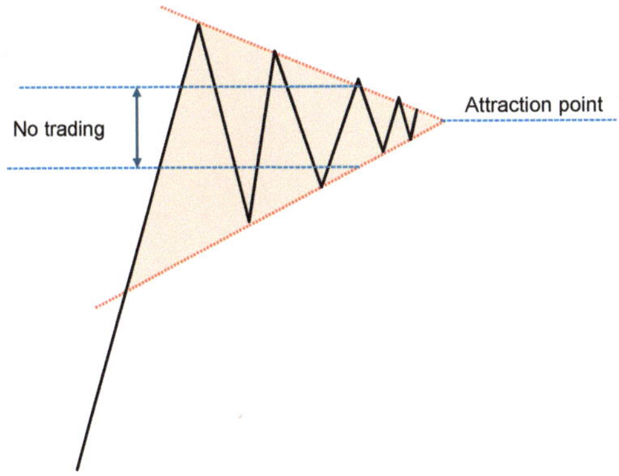

7.3.1 BUY AND SELL AREAS

Wait for the price to separate from the middle of the triangle.

Look for long entries under the attraction point and for short entries above the attraction point.

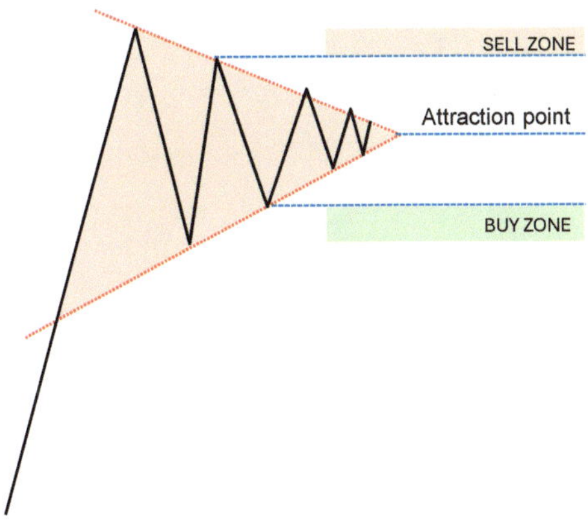

Ideal buy and sell zones in a triangle.

The best areas for an entry are always **traps at swing highs or swing lows.**

Target prices will be as follows:

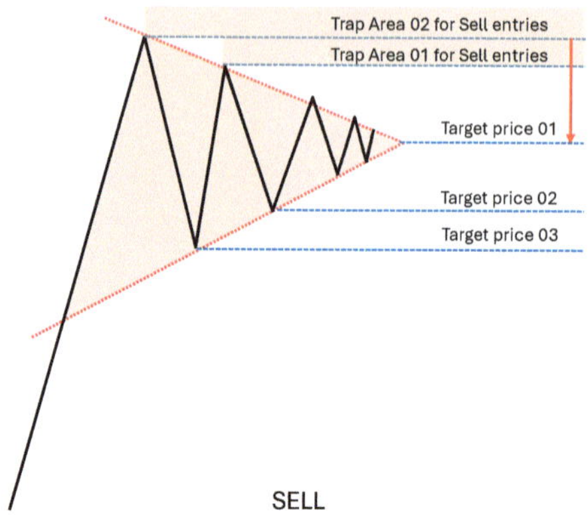

7.3.2 Entry pattern / signal

Depending on the direction of the previous momentum you will be looking for a W or VW Pattern:

If you trade **in the same direction** of the overall momentum, use a **W Pattern.**

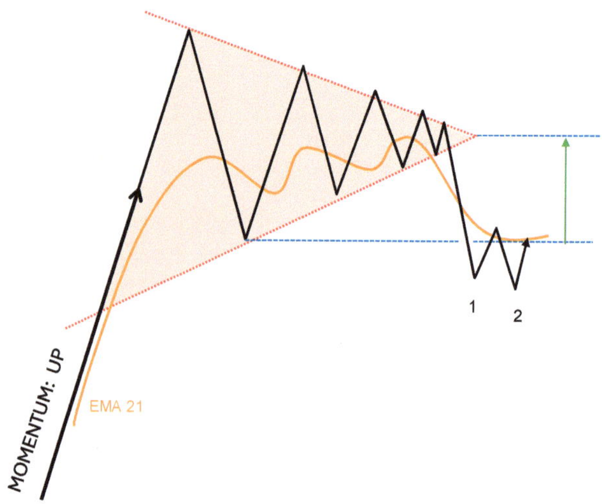

If you trade **against the direction** of the overall momentum, use an inverted **WV Pattern.**

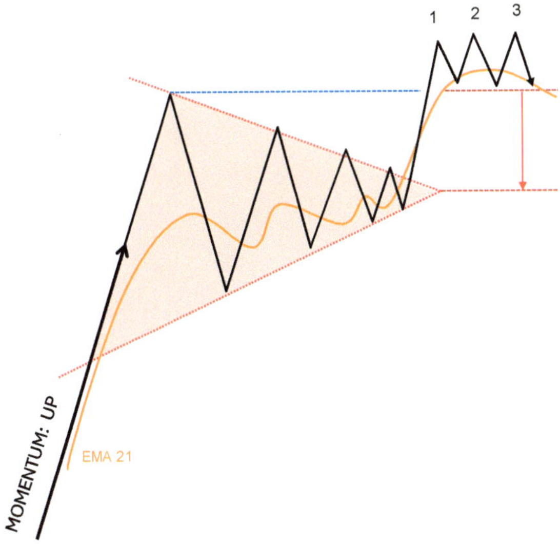

A triangle pattern and trades (long and short) using W patterns. The middle of the triangle is a reliable place for the 1st target price.

Example of triangle pattern, with a W pattern as entry signal in a downtrend. PDD stock, 1 min chart.

7.4 PULLBACKS AT A MAJOR SUPPORT LEVEL (UPTREND)

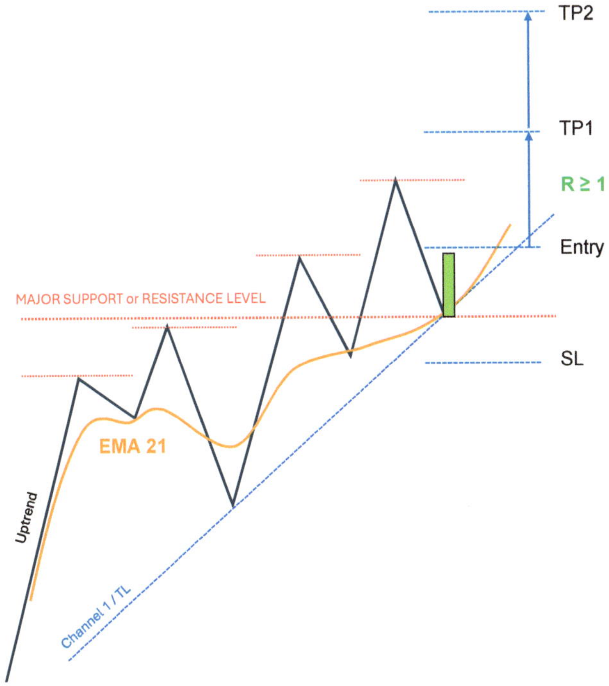

Characteristics

- There must be a previous uptrend.
- The best ones occur around a confluence zone, where different support and resistance levels intersect.
- EMA 21 crosses the major support or resistance level.
- Signal candle (pin bar or strong candle) coming from the EMA 21.

How to trade them

- Look for a signal candle like a pin bar or an engulfing candle.
- The price magnet is the next measured move, see Chapter 5.2.

Important details

- There must be enough space between your entry level and the next resistance level (or trendline). Look for a risk-reward ratio (RR) greater than 1.
- For a long position, the signal candle must be a strong one (no wick on top).

Example of a pullback pattern. ES futures contract. 1000 tick chart.

IF THE PULLBACK PATTERN APPEARS AT A TRAP LEVEL, IT IS A HIGH-PROBABILITY WINNING TRADE

Example of some pullback patterns bouncing off EMA 21 in a downtrend.

Micron stock. 1min chart.

7.5 RUNS

7.5.1 RUN AND CHANNEL

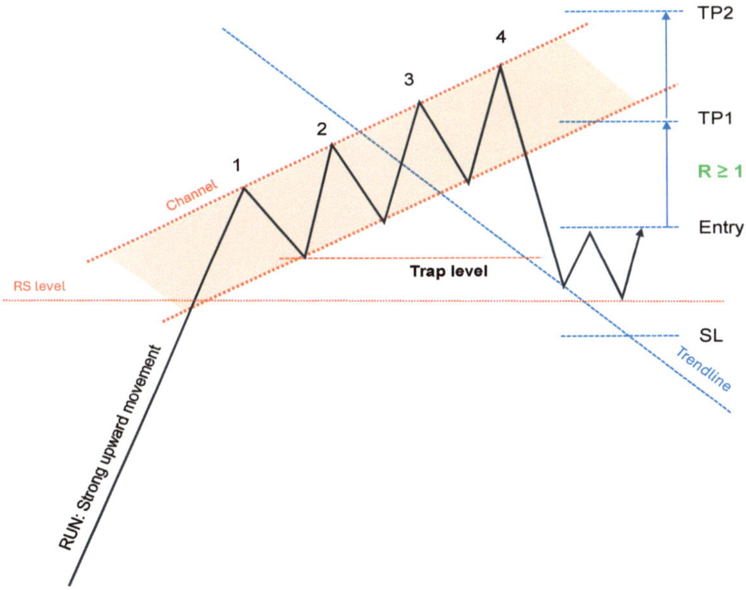

Characteristics

- One strong move up.
- Formation of a channel with price retesting 3-4 times the channel top line.
- Wait for a full retracement back to the base of the channel (the trap level).

How to trade them

- Look for an entry signal at that trap level: whether it is a W pattern or a strongly closing candle.
- First target price at RR=1.
- Last target price at the top of the channel.

Important details

- There must be enough space between your entry level and the first resistance level, at least a RR=1.

- If the retracement is a 2-legged one or there is a trendline coming down, look for entries above the formed trendline, see Chapter 7.1.1.

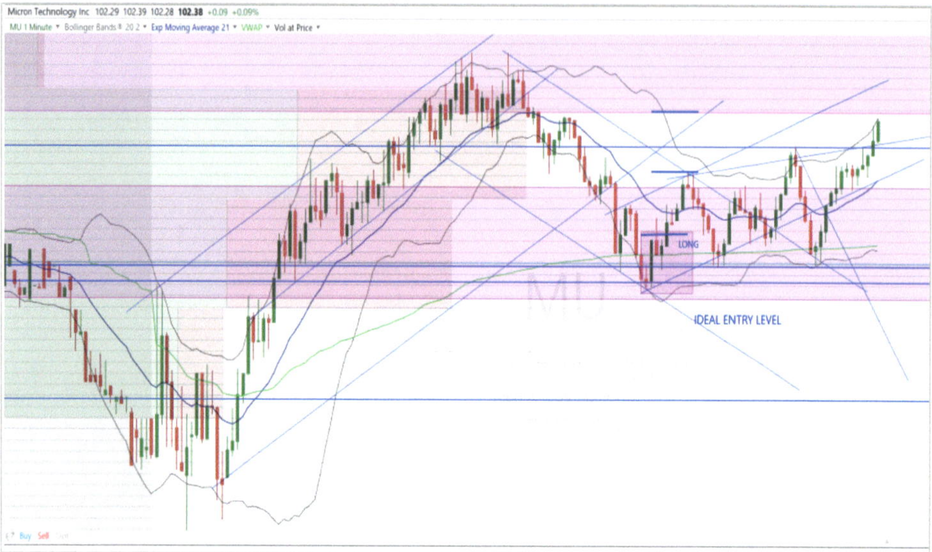

Example of Run and channel pattern. W pattern as entry signal. Micron stock 1min chart.

Example of "run and channel pattern" and inverted WV pattern as entry signal. ES futures contract. 1000 tick chart.

7.5.2 Ray and Trap

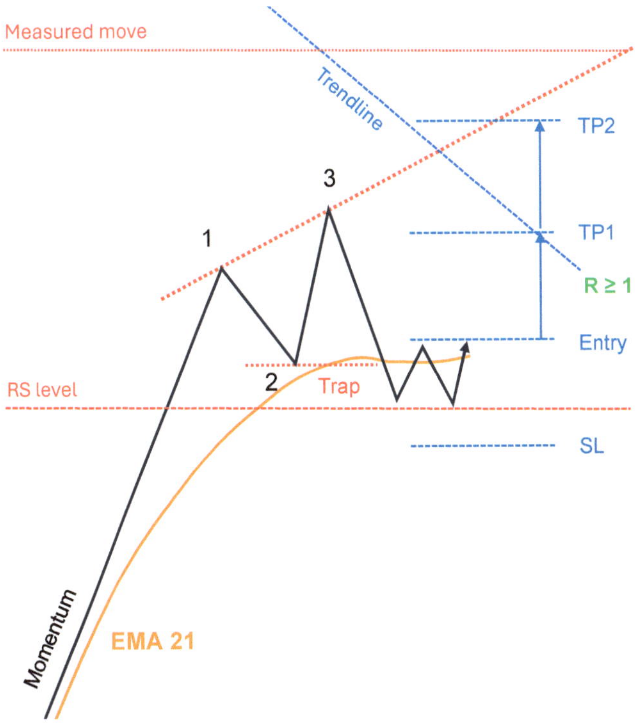

Characteristics

- One-legged strong move up.
- Formation of a higher swing high (marker 3 higher than marker 1).
- The swing low (marker 2) doesn't touch EMA 21. This is important.
- Retracement against the trend.
- Price crossing below EMA 21.

"RAY AND TRAPS" ARE HIGH-PROBABILITY TRADE SETUPS

How to trade them

- Price must cross the trap level. Wait for a retracement to the trap level.
- Look for an entry signal at that trap level:

  Option 1: a W pattern.

  Option 2: a quick, strong candle closing at EMA 21.

- Place the first target price slightly below the price level indicated by marker 3.

Important details

- There must be enough space between your entry level and the next resistance level (or trendline). Look for a risk-reward ratio greater than 1:1.
- If the retracement is a 2-legged one or there is a trendline coming down, look for entries above the formed trendline, as explained in Chapter 7.1.1.

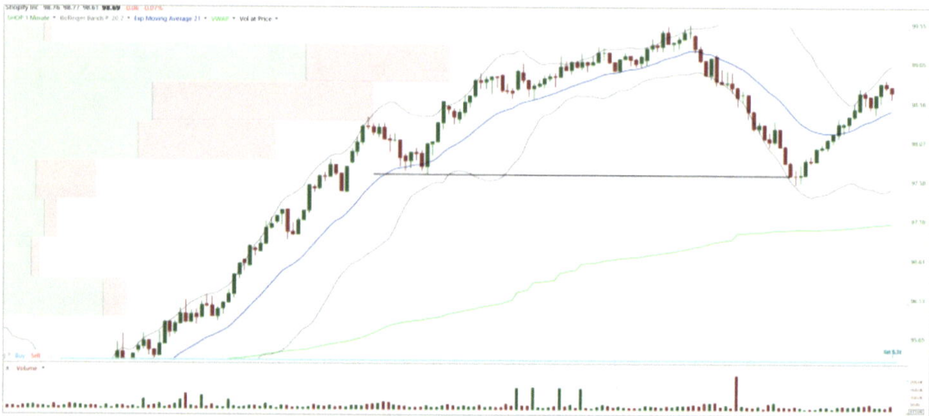

Example of "ray and trap" in an uptrend. SHOP stock, 1 min chart.

Example of "ray and trap" in an uptrend. ES futures contract.

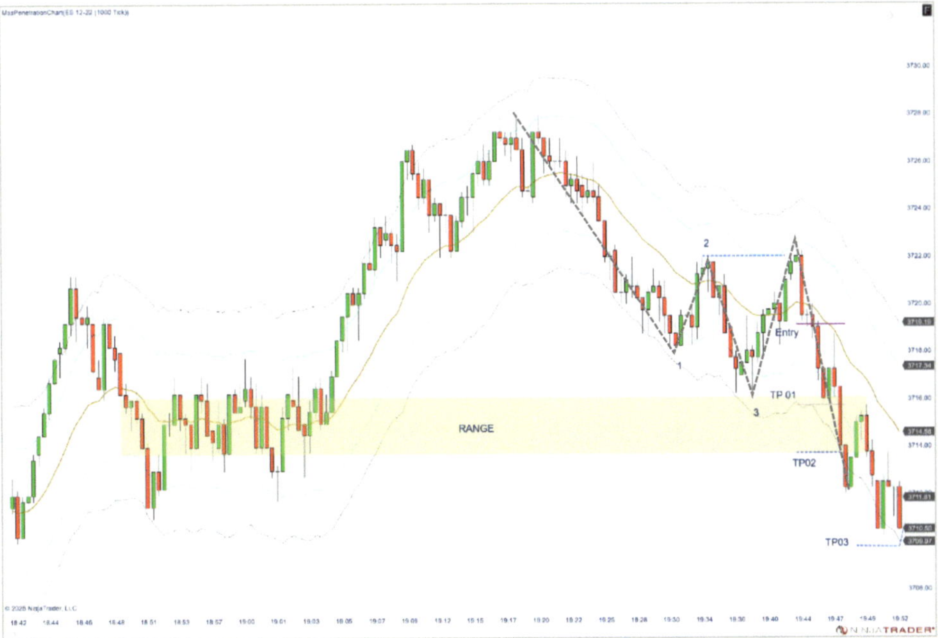

Example of "ray and trap" in a downtrend. ES futures contract.

7.6 FLAGS

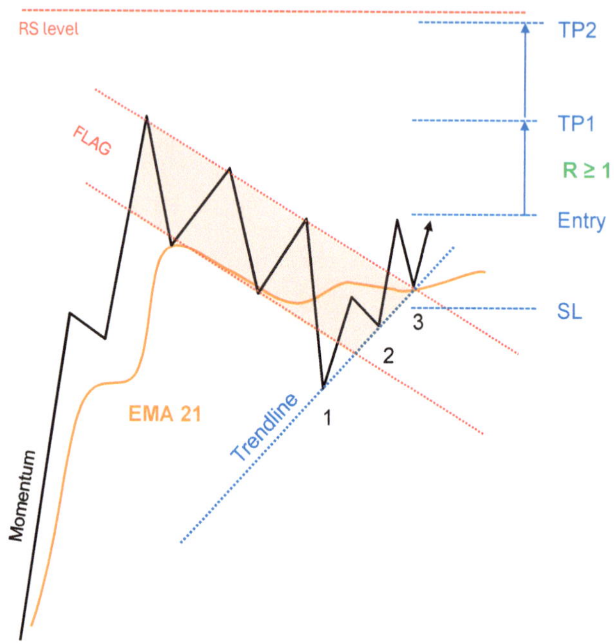

Characteristics

- Previous momentum upward.
- Flag (channel coming down).
- 3 Retests of the trendline.
- Last retest with confluence at the top of the flag. (look for a level with strong confluence).
- EMA 21 crossing the top line of the flag pattern.

How to trade them

- Wait for a signal candle (like a pin bar or an engulfing candle) bouncing off the EMA 21 (see marker 3).
- Price magnet is the next measured move, see Chapter 5.2.
- First target price at RR=1.
- Last target price at the top of the channel.

Important details

- There must be enough space between your entry level and the next resistance level (or trendline). Look for a risk-reward (RR) > 1.
- Ideally, the signal candle must be strong (no wick on top).

Example of a Flag pattern and a WV entry pattern.

Sometimes your entry signal will be a W pattern appearing at the top line of the flag. Wait for a confluence zone, where the EMA 21, a trendline and the top line of the flag come together.

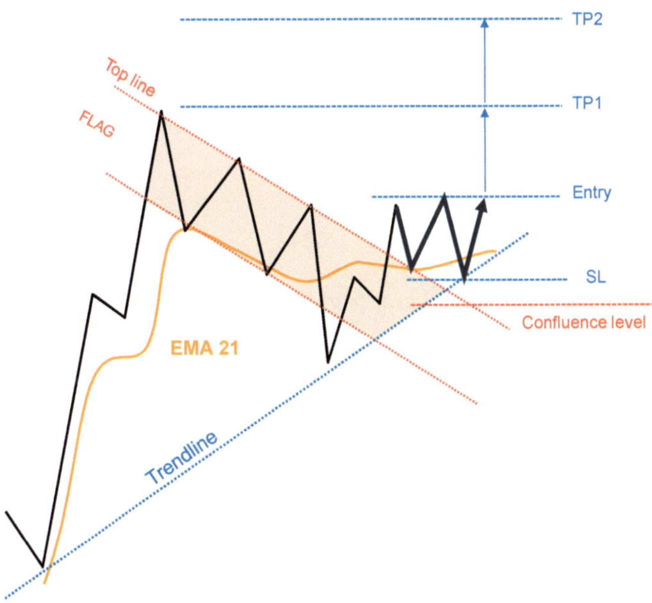

7.7 WEDGES

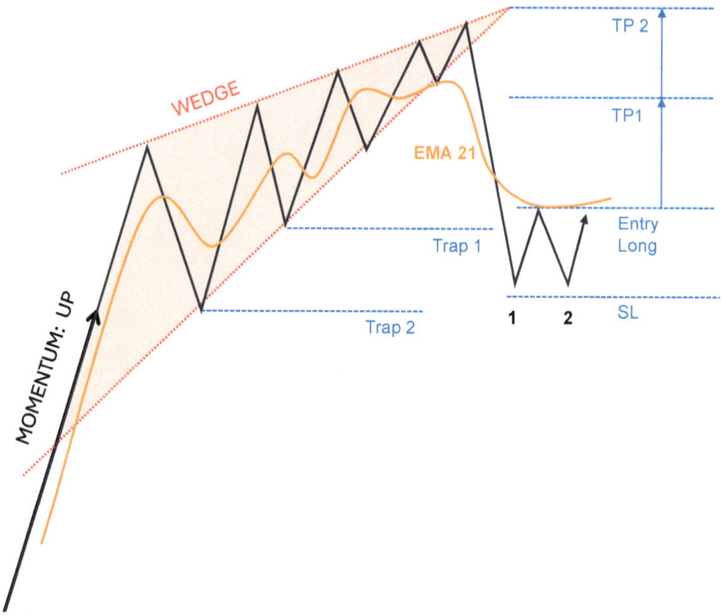

Characteristics

- Previous momentum upward.
- Wedge pattern.
- If the wedge is getting tight, meaning there is no more space inside the wedge for a trade, wait for a retracement.
- Mark possible trap levels.
- Wait for price to retest a trap level.

How to trade them

- Look for an entry signal at a trap level:

  Option 1: a W pattern.

  Option 2: a quick, strong candle closing at EMA 21.

- First target price at RR=1.
- Final target price slightly below the end of the wedge.

Example of a wedge pattern. W pattern (after a retracement to a trap level) as entry signal. ES futures contract. 1000 tick chart.

7.7.1 How to trade inside wedges

Don't trade inside the wedge if it is too tight. In case of wider wedges look for trades at the top line of the wedge, in a downtrend, or at the bottom line in an uptrend movement.

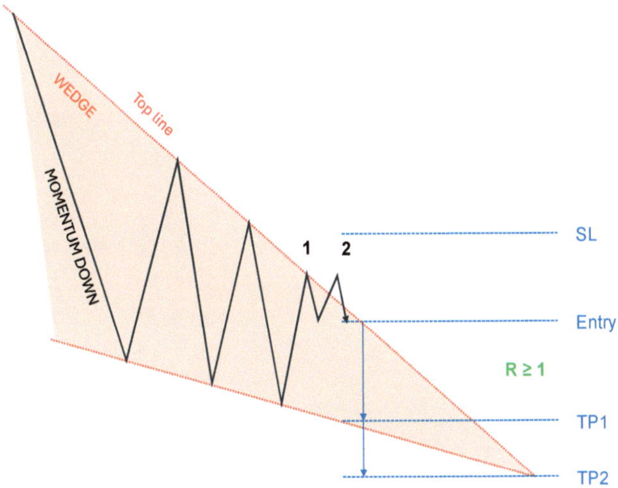

Strategy for a downtrend, inside a wedge pattern. W pattern at the top line.

Characteristics

- Previous condition: momentum downward.
- Wedge pattern.
- Wait for a retest of the wedge top line (we look for a short position, if the main movement is downward).
- Only enter the trade, if there is enough space inside the wedge for a trade with RR > 1.

How to trade them

- Look for an entry signal after the retest of the wedge top line:

  Option 1: a W pattern.

  Option 2: a quick strong candle closing at the EMA 21.

- First target price (TP1) at RR=1.
- Final target price (TP2) slightly above the end of the wedge.

Example of a trade inside a wedge in a downtrend movement.

7.8 REVERSAL PATTERNS

7.8.1 COMPLEX TRAP REVERSAL

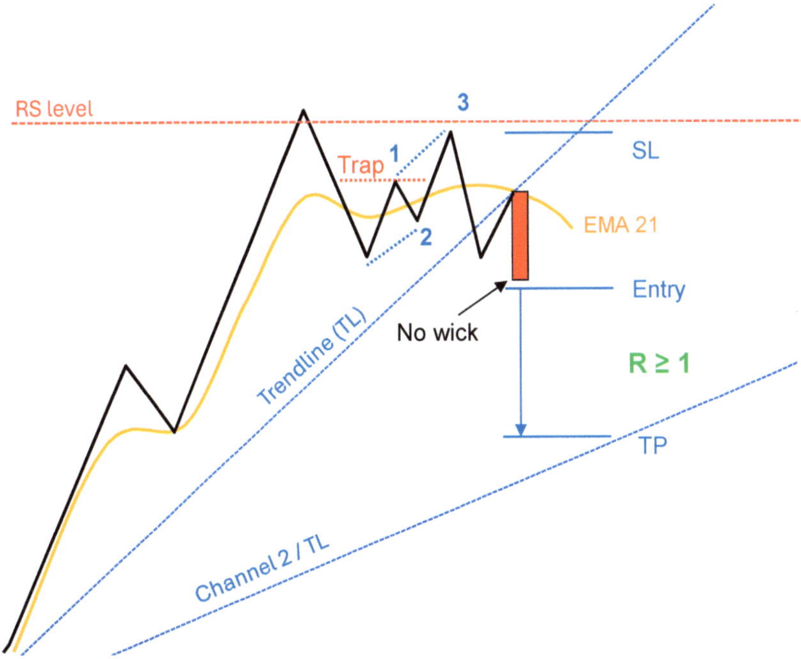

Conditions of a complex trap reversal (up-down).

Characteristics

- It can also be seen as a W pattern failing.
- The reversal pattern must contain a small 123 pattern in the same direction as the previous momentum.
- A trap must appear in the opposite direction.
- Price crosses below EMA 21.
- A strong candle indicates that a reversal might be in place.

How to trade them

- If there is a trendline (TL) coming up, wait for price to cross the trendline as well as for a retest of the trendline. The entry signal will be a big strong candle (ideally without a wick).
- In you want to be conservative and reduce risk, you can use a limit order to enter the trade, as explained in Chapter 10.1 and 10.2.

Example of complex trap reversal (up-down). ES futures contract.

Example of a complex trap reversal (down-up), ES futures contract. 1000 tick chart.

7.8.2 PERSISTENCE CHANNEL

7.8.2.1 *Entry under the channel: Capitulation*

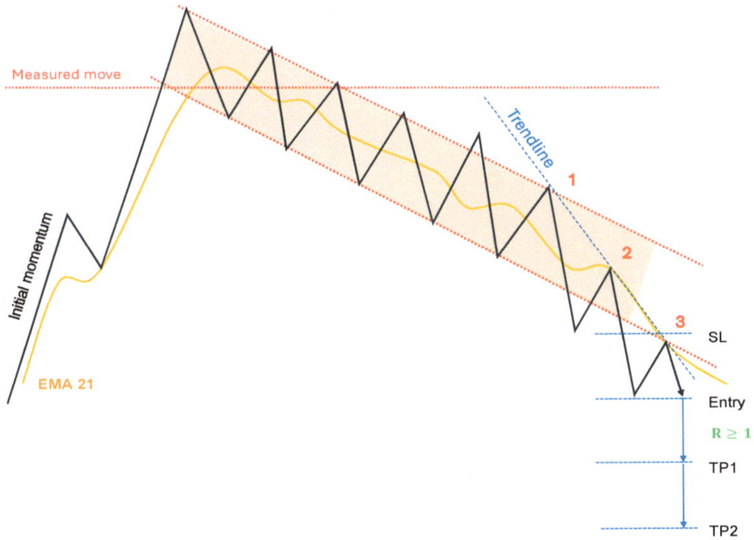

Characteristics

- Channel coming down in the opposite direction of the initial momentum.
- The channel must be narrow.
- Buyers will try many times to push price higher without success.
- It feels as if an algorithm is controlling the price, as the channel will have a very accurate geometry.
- After many bounces back and forth, price will move along a trendline, bouncing 3 times down.

How to trade them

- At the 3rd bounce off the trendline, look for an entry signal (usually a strong candle or a pin bar) bouncing off the bottom line of the channel (see the setup for a short trade in the image above).

Important

- Persistence channels can be misleading because their strong signal candles can falsely suggest high-quality entries against the prevailing direction.Don't get confused when you see them.

Example of persistance channel and entry short after 3 tries down.

Example of a persistence channel. An engulfing pattern fails to reverse price upward, highlighting strong downward pressure.

STRONG CANDLES AGAINST THE DIRECTION OF THE PERSISTENCE CHANNEL ARE NOT A RELIABLE REVERSAL SIGNAL

Example of a smaller persistence channel (inclined range).

7.8.2.2 Entry above the channel: Trap at previous swing high

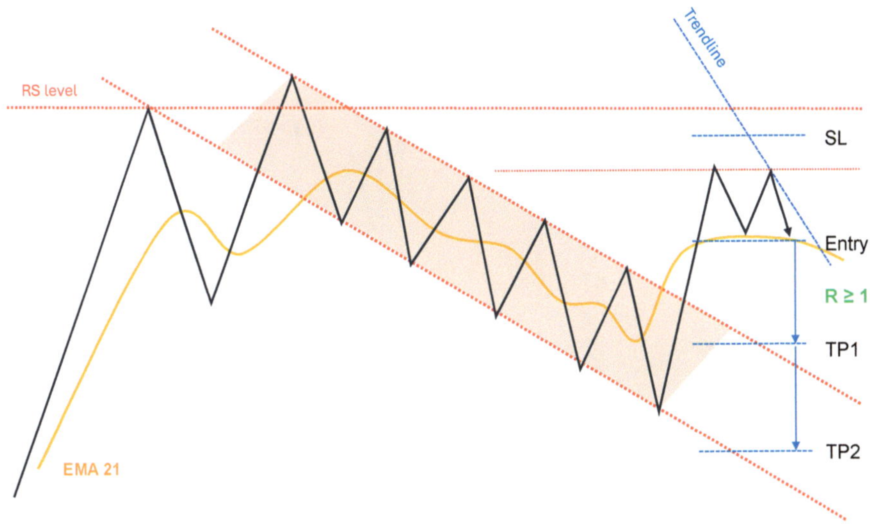

In some cases price will move upward, break above the channel and then fall back down again to the persistence channel, which acts as a magnet. You can trade this pattern by waiting for an inverted W formation, at a confluence level.

Example of a persistence channel in a downtrend movement, with a short entry at an inverted W pattern.

Example of a persistence channel in an uptrend. ES futures contract. Entry signal above trendline coming down.

PERSISTENCE CHANNELS CAN BE VERY PROFITABLE, AS THEY ARE SOMETIMES FOLLOWED BY A LARGER MOVE

7.8.3 3 x 3 Tries reversal

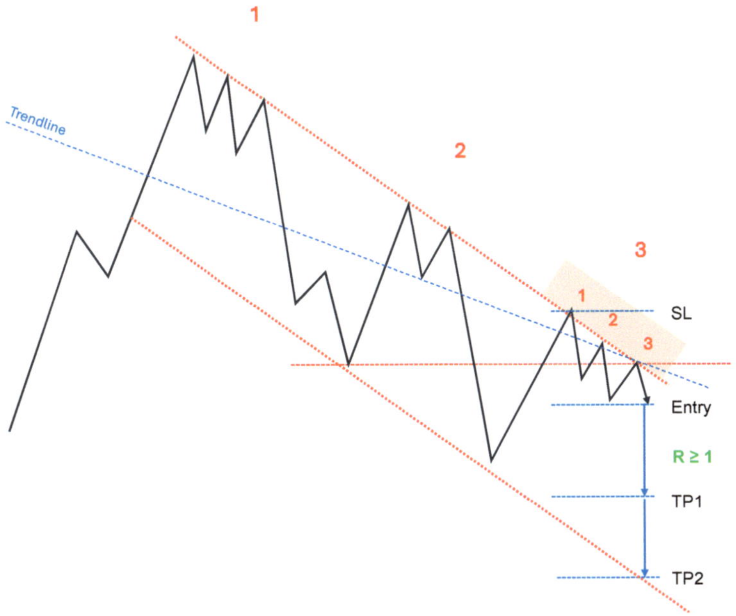

Characteristics

What you need to see is a pattern composed of 3 major swings (or peaks) along a trendline, where the final major peak itself is formed by 3 minor swings.

Example of 3 x 3 tries reversal pattern.

Interpretation of the pattern

This pattern occurs when market participants repeatedly attempt to push price upward, but a "hidden force" prevents it from breaking above a well-defined trendline. These types of reversals are quite common, reliable, and often profitable, as many traders capitulate after multiple failed attempts.

Example of 3x3 tries reversal pattern. ES futures contract. 1000 tick chart.

7.8.4 CLIMAX REVERSAL: PARABOLIC MOVEMENT

Example of parabolic movement. ES futures contract. 1000 tick chart.

Characteristics

Parabolic moves can signal the end of a trend, at least in the short term, especially when accompanied by high volume and occurring at the 3rd or 4th measured move (MM). Parabolic moves, as the name suggests, follow a curved trajectory (parabolic shape), with candles increasing in size as the move accelerates, typically forming at the end of an extended trend

How to trade them

- Look for a confluence level, where different trendlines and resistance levels converge.
- The RSI indicator can also help confirm the end of a downward parabolic move when it drops below 10 (for upward parabolic moves, RSI values above 80 may suggest price is overextended and that a short-term reversal is likely to happen).
- They are usually accompanied by a surge in volume and volatility.

Example of a parabolic move downward. BABA stock 1min chart.

7.8.4.1 Difference between a falling knife and a parabolic movement

The key difference between a "falling knife" and a parabolic move lies not only in the geometry but also in the meaning of the move.

A **falling knife** is a sharp decline in price, typically in a straight line, driven by panic or negative news. It signals strong momentum in one direction, and you never know when it ends. Trying to predict the end of a falling knife is very risky.

Example of a falling knife.

The geometry of a **parabolic pattern** involves a steep, downward price curve that accelerates as momentum builds. Price declines gradually at first, then steepens into a near-vertical drop.

Parabolic movement.

A similar price movement, but with a completely different meaning is when price bounces off EMA 21 multiple times, see chart below. This movement represents a sustainable downtrend, which might continue for a long time.

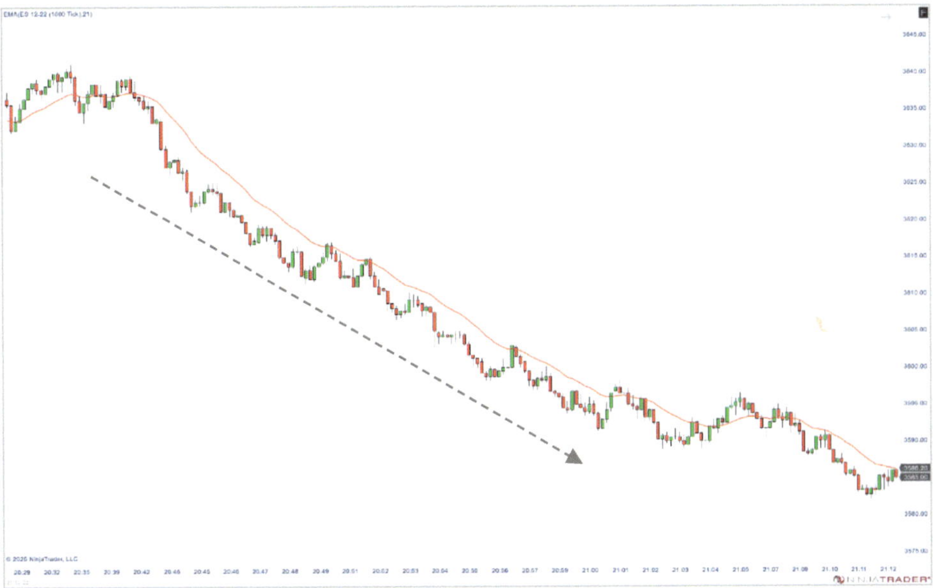

7.9 GAPS

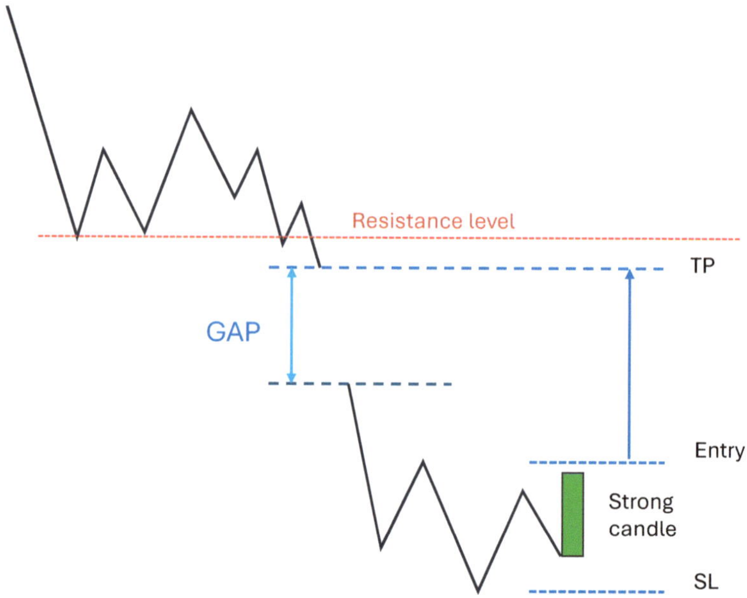

In trading, gaps can indeed act as attraction points, commonly referred to as "gap-fill" or "gap-close" areas. A gap occurs when the price of a financial instrument opens significantly higher or lower than the previous day's closing price, creating a visible empty space on the price chart.

When a gap is formed, it often becomes a point of interest for traders because prices tend to gravitate towards these unfilled gaps, attempting to "fill" or "close" them. However…

NOT ALL GAPS GET FILLED IMMEDIATELY

In some cases, a gap can also indicate strong momentum in one direction. In such scenarios, a gap may be treated as the beginning of a trend rather than just a price imbalance.

Example of a gap signaling strong downward momentum.

7.10 FAILURES

7.10.1 EVEN THE BEST STRATEGY CAN FAIL

We call it a failure, when a high probability strategy fails. That's often the signal to exit the trade. But it's more than just a warning; it can also be an opportunity.

When a widely anticipated setup fails, the resulting move is often driven by a wave of triggered stop-losses. By entering a trade in the opposite direction, you can ride that momentum.

In fact, it can even be worth **doubling your position size** in the opposite direction, as these failure patterns often lead to sharp, extended moves driven by trapped traders exiting their positions.

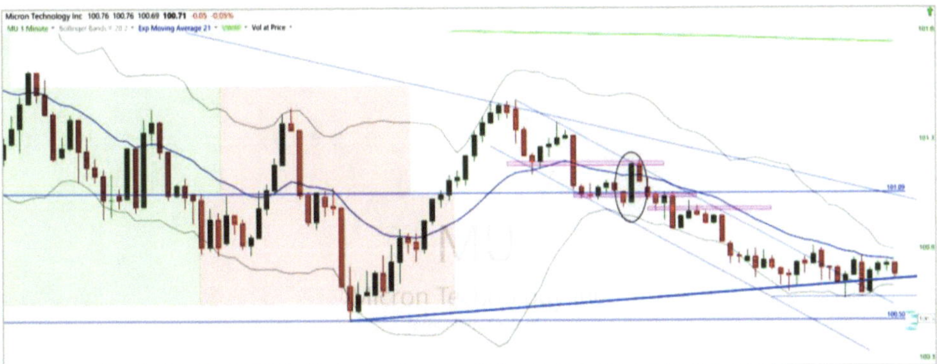

Example of a strong green candle at support level failing.

7.10.2 Failure examples

7.10.2.1 Descending triangle breakout failing

Pattern confirming a continuation of the trend: entry of trapped traders

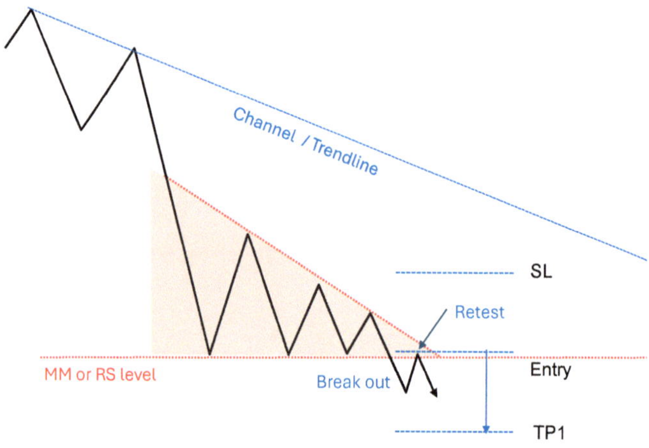

Descending triangle breakout and entry short after retest of the breakout level.

Pattern failing and reversing the trend: trading the failure setup

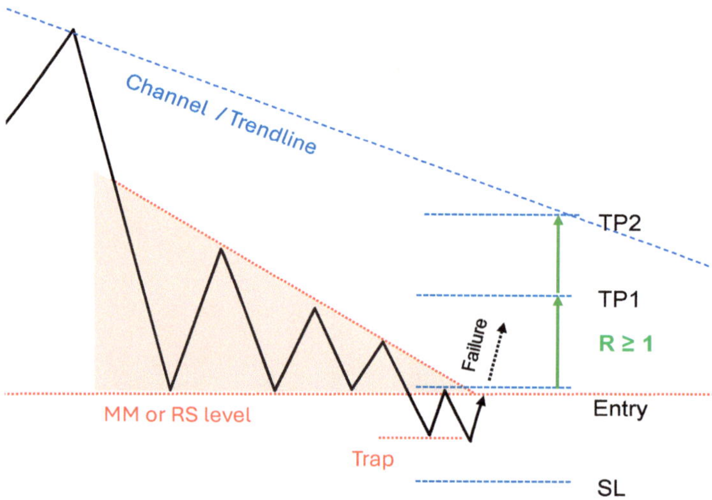

Descending triangle breakout failing.

Example of a descending triangle breakout failing (down-up). PDD stock, 1min chart.

7.10.2.2 Flag failure

Pattern confirming a continuation of the trend: entry of trapped traders

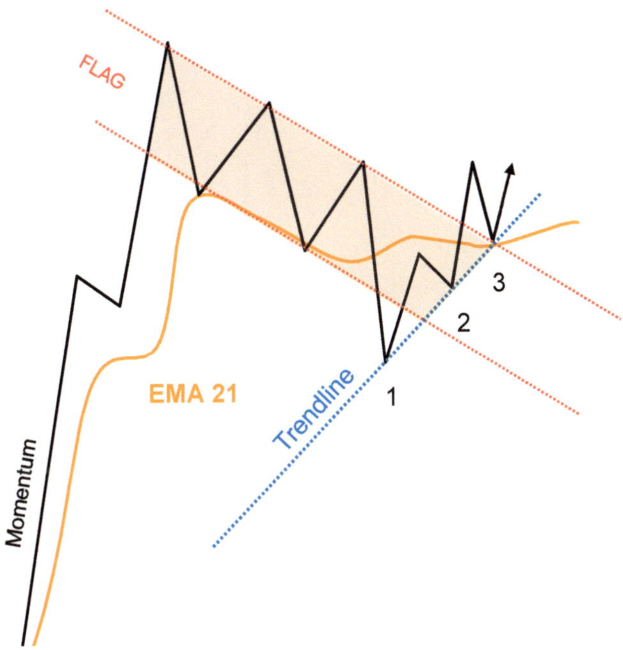

Narrow flag breakout.

Pattern failing and reversing the trend: trading the failure setup

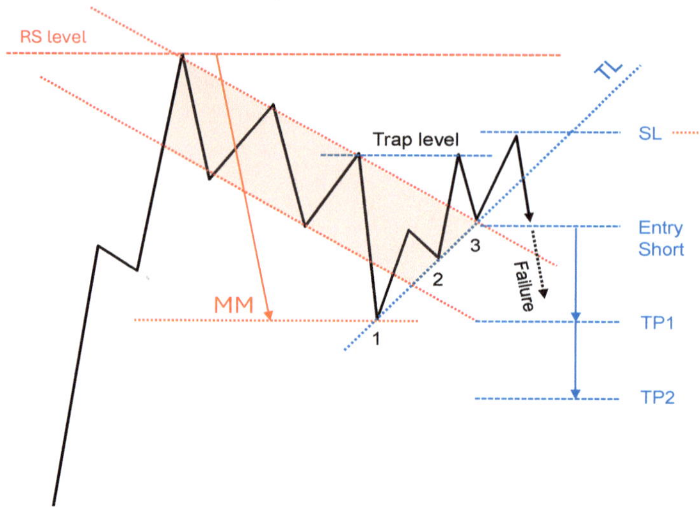

Failure (up-down) of a narrow flag breakout.

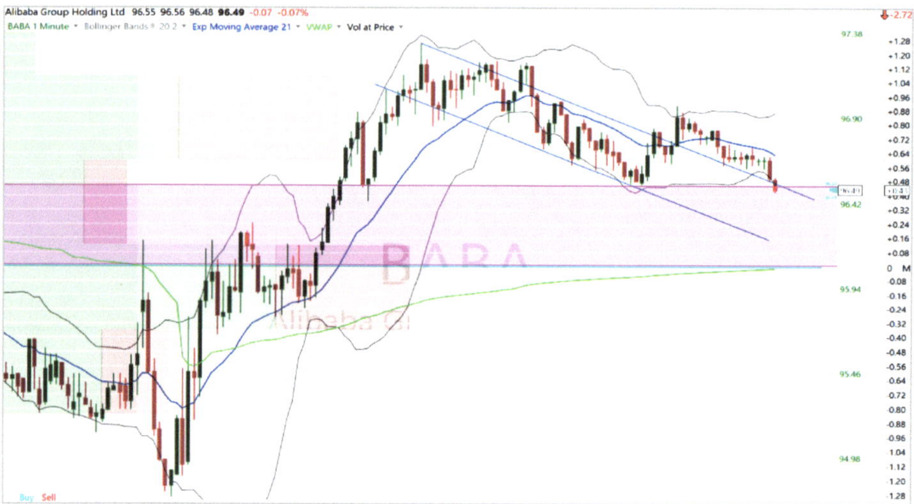

Example of a flag pattern failure (up-down). BABA stock, 1min chart.

7.10.2.3 Complex trap reversal failing

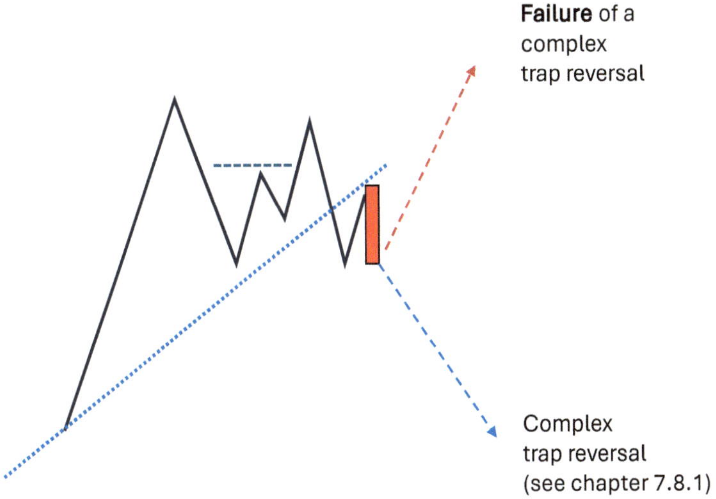

Complex trap reversal (see Chapter 7.8.1) and failure of a trap reversal.

Example of a complex trap reversal failing. ES futures contract. 1000 tick chart.

7.10.2.4 Good-looking signal candles can fail

Example of a strong signal candle (engulfing candle) failing.

The move downward is too strong. As we said previously, candlestick patterns are not enough.

8 CORRELATIONS AND DEPENDENCY

In the stock market, correlation refers to the statistical relationship between the price movements of two or more assets. A positive correlation means that as one asset's price increases, the other tends to rise as well, while a negative correlation indicates that when one asset rises, the other falls or vice versa.

8.1 CORRELATION TO MAJOR INDEXES

Price movements of an individual stock or sector relate to the performance of broader market indices, such as the S&P 500, Dow Jones Industrial Average, or NASDAQ. Based on this phenomenon, it is possible to develop strategies to forecast the price movement of certain financial instruments.

8.1.1 WHY DOES CORRELATION WORK?

Market sentiment is the overall mood of investors, whether they feel confident (bullish) or fearful (bearish). This collective emotion strongly influences stock prices. When investors are worried, they tend to sell, pushing prices down. This effect is especially noticeable in major indexes like the S&P 500 or NASDAQ.

8.1.2 WHY MARKET WEAKNESS OFTEN SPREADS ACROSS STOCKS

- **Investor psychology and herd behavior.**
  When people see the market falling, they often panic and follow others in selling to avoid further losses. This herd mentality causes a snowball effect, leading to more selling and lower prices.

- **Institutional selling.**
  Institutional investors often follow strict risk management rules that limit allowable losses. When losses reach a set threshold, these rules may force them to sell assets to reduce exposure. This selling isn't always based on fundamentals but rather on pre-defined limits, which can accelerate market declines during downturns.

- **Algorithmic and passive trading.**
  Many automated trading systems react to movements in major indices.

A drop in the NASDAQ or S&P 500 can trigger automatic sell orders, which puts even more pressure on stock prices.

A DROP IN THE NASDAQ 100 OR S&P 500 SIGNALS BROAD MARKET WEAKNESS. IT MIGHT SET OFF A CHAIN REACTION OF FEAR, LARGE-SCALE SELLING BY INSTITUTIONS, AND ALGORITHMIC TRADING, CAUSING MOST STOCKS TO FALL IN CORRELATION WITH THE INDEX.

8.2 HOW TO USE CORRELATION BETWEEN STOCKS

When trading a stock, it's useful to look for correlations with similar stocks in the same industry and analyze how their price movements relate.

For example, if you're trading **Micron (MU)**, you might use **Nvidia (NVDA)** as a reference point. Both companies operate within the semiconductor sector, and their stock prices often exhibit a similar behavior and even similar patterns.

By comparing the price charts of both stocks, you may notice that their swings, both upward and downward, tend to occur around the same time. In some cases, one stock may react slightly earlier than the other, allowing you to anticipate the direction of the next price movement.

This relationship can provide valuable insight:

IF NVIDIA BEGINS TO MOVE BEFORE MICRON, THAT EARLY ACTION MIGHT SERVE AS A SIGNAL TO ANTICIPATE A SIMILAR MOVE IN MICRON, HELPING YOU TO MAKE MORE INFORMED TRADING DECISIONS.

Micron stock.

Nvidia stock.

At 12pm and around 1:20pm both stocks formed a swing high and the price movement of both stocks was almost identical (see images below)

AMD Stock.

NVDA Stock.

Micron Stock.

Example of correlation. Semiconductor stocks moving in the same direction. NVDA, Micron and AMD stocks.

9 RISK MANAGEMENT

Risk management is your trading survival kit, without it, even the most brilliant strategy can fall apart.

Think of it as your personal defense system in the markets. It's not just about avoiding losses, it's about controlling them, staying in the game, and letting your winners run when the opportunity is right. In trading, losses are inevitable.

What separates successful traders from the rest isn't the absence of losing trades, but how they manage risk when things don't go as planned.

Proper risk management starts with **position sizing**, never risking more than a small percentage of your capital on a single trade. Combine that with **stop-loss orders** to cap downside, and you're already miles ahead of most beginners. But there's more: **diversify your trades**, don't chase revenge trades, and always evaluate the **risk-to-reward ratio** before entering a position.

It's tempting to focus on entries and signals, but risk management is what keeps you in the game long enough to let your edge play out. Without it, even a high win-rate strategy can crash your account. With it, you can trade with confidence, clarity, and consistency, and that's where long-term success lives.

9.1 RISK-REWARD RATIO (RR)

The most important parameter of any trade is the risk-reward ratio. It measures the potential profit of a trade relative to its potential loss. It helps you evaluate whether a trade is worth taking.

$$Risk - Reward\ Ratio = \frac{Potential\ Gain}{Potential\ Loss} = \frac{Target\ price - Entry}{Entry - Stop\ loss}$$

If you risk \$100 to potentially make \$300, the risk-reward ratio is:

$$\frac{Potential\ Gain}{Potentail\ Loss} = 1 : 3$$

This means, for every $1 risked, you aim to gain $3. We also say that the trade has a risk-reward ratio of 3.

$$RR = 3$$

A good risk-reward ratio depends on the strategy you use. You should aim for a RR of 2 to stay profitable over time.

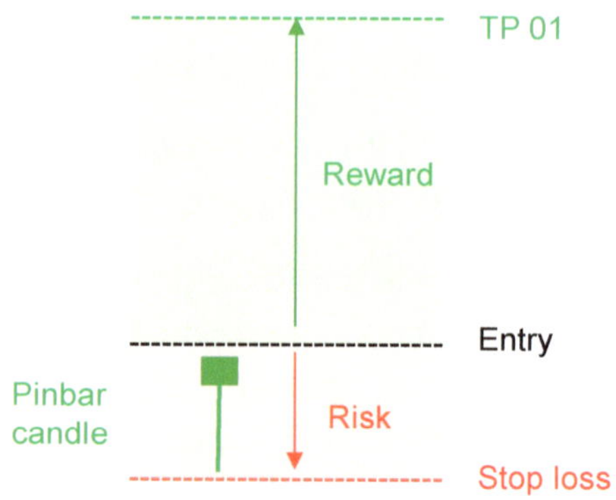

RR = Reward / Risk

9.2 PNL

The PnL (Profit and Loss) refers to the financial result of a trade, trading period, or portfolio over time. It measures how much money has been made (profit) or lost (loss).

The risk-reward ratio (RR) is a better way to evaluate trades than just looking at the PnL because it focuses on trade quality rather than short-term monetary outcomes.

PnL can be misleading, a $100 profit might look great, but if you risked $500, it's not a good trade. Conversely, a $500 loss might seem bad, but if the RR was 5, it was a well-planned trade.

> ***THE RISK-REWARD RATIO MEASURES EFFICIENCY, CONSISTENCY, AND LONG-TERM SUSTAINABILITY OF YOUR TRADING STRATEGY, WHILE THE PNL ONLY SHOWS SHORT-TERM RESULTS***

9.3 POSITION SIZING

Position sizing determines how much capital you should allocate on each trade. A common approach is the fixed percentage method, where you risk a certain percentage of your trading account per trade - usually 0,5% to 2% depending on your experience, the strategies you use and your risk tolerance.

9.3.1 HOW TO CALCULATE THE NUMBER OF STOCKS TO TRADE

To calculate the number of stocks to trade based on your account size, you should consider risk management and position sizing. Here's a step-by-step approach:

1. Define your risk per trade (% of account size)

Most traders risk 1-2% of their total account per trade to manage losses.

- Example: If you have a $10,000 account and risk 1% per trade, your max risk per trade is:

$$\$10{,}000 \times 0.01 = \$100$$

You should not lose more than $100 on a single trade.

2. Determine your stop-loss distance (risk per share)

This is the difference between your entry price and your stop-loss price.

- Example:
  - Buy stock at $10.05
  - Stop-loss at $9.85 (usually below your entry signal)
  - Risk per share = $10.05 - $9.85 = $0.20 per share

3. Calculate position size (number of shares to trade)

Use this formula:

$$Number\ of\ shares = \frac{Risk\ per\ trade}{Risk\ per\ share}$$

Using the previous example:

$$100 / 0.20 = 500 \text{ shares}$$

You should buy 500 shares to stay within your risk limit.

Example of a RR calculation for a stock:

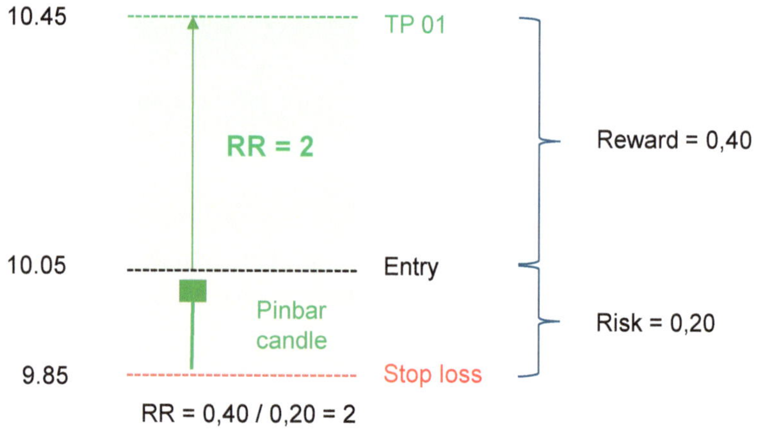

Summarizing:

- If your account is $10,000.
- Your risk is 1% of your account per trade.
- Your risk per trade is $100.
- The right stop-loss (SL) to protect your trade must be under your entry signal. The size of the stop-loss only depends on the ATR14 and on the quality of your entry.
- In this case the SL is $0.20 away from your entry level, right under the wick of a green pin bar. It defines the maximal loss per trade if you bought just one stock.
- You aim for a RR=2, meaning your target price (TP) is 0.20 x 2 = $0.40 away from your entry.
- The number of stocks to trade depends on the SL position, on your account size and on the taken risk: as you want to risk $100 per trade and the maximal loss per trade (for one stock is $0.20). In this case you will be buying 500 stocks (100 / 0.20 = 500 stocks).
- The price of the stock at the entry point is $10.05, which means you will need to invest a total amount of $5,025 (= $10.05 x 500) to execute the trade, according to the previous parameters.
- If you lose, you will be losing $100 (measured in RR, you will be losing -1R)
- If you win, you will be winning $200 (measured in RR, you will be winning +2R)

9.3.2 How to calculate the number of futures contracts to trade

Position sizing in futures trading differs significantly from stock trading because of how the contracts are structured and how leverage is applied.

When trading stocks, position size is typically calculated based on the price per share and the amount of capital you're willing to risk. For example, if a stock is trading at $50 and you want to invest $5,000, you can simply buy 100 shares.

In futures trading, however, you're not buying shares, you're trading contracts, each with a specific value tied to an underlying asset (like oil, gold, or the S&P 500). You don't pay the full contract value upfront. Instead, you post margin, which is a fraction of the total value, allowing for high leverage.

To size your position in futures, you need to calculate:

1. **The tick value** – how much you gain or lose per tick (the smallest price movement of the futures contract).
2. **The stop-loss size in ticks** – how far you're willing to let the price move against you in ticks.
3. **The dollar risk per trade** – how much you're willing to lose on the trade.

Then you can determine how many contracts to trade based on your risk tolerance. These are the steps you should follow:

1. Define your risk per trade (% of account size)

You should risk 0,5 - 2% of your total account per trade.

Example:

If your account is $50,000 and you risk 1% per trade, your max risk per trade is: $ 50,000 × 0.01 = $ 500

You should not lose more than $500 on a single trade.

2. Determine the risk per contract

Futures contracts have a tick size and a tick value, which determine how much money is gained or lost per price movement.

A TICK IS THE SMALLEST PRICE MOVEMENT OF A FUTURES CONTRACT ON THE CHART

And for each future contract, a tick has a different value in $.

The tick value and size are different for each future contract. These are the most common ones:

Future contract	Symbol	Tick value ($)	Tick size
E mini S&P	ES	12,50	0,25
E mini Nasdaq	NQ	5,00	0,25
Micro E mini S&P	MES	1,25	0,25
Micro E mini Nasdaq	MNQ	0,5	0,25
Crude Oil	CL	10	0,1
Gold	GC	10	0,01

For example, a tick value = $12.50 per contract means that for every one-tick movement in price, the profit or loss changes by $12.50 for a single contract.

It is also common to use points instead of ticks as a unit for the price movement. A point is made up of multiple ticks, depending on the instrument. For example in the E-mini S&P 500 (ES), one point equals four ticks. Since each tick is worth $12.50, one full point is worth $50 per contract.

FOR THE E-MINI S&P 500: 1 POINT = 4 TICKS

Example trading the E-mini S&P 500 Future (ES):

- Tick size = 0.25 points (1 point = 4 ticks).
- Tick value = $12.50 per contract.
- Let us assume you need a stop-loss distance of 2 points (8 ticks) to protect your trade.
- Risk per contract is 8 ticks × $12.50 = $100

With each contract you risk **$100**.

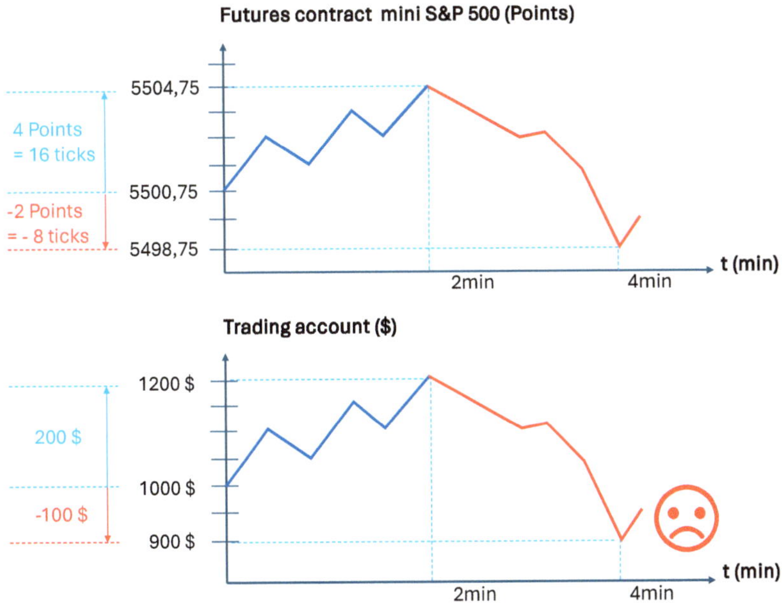

Illustration of how the dollar value of a trade evolves in the S&P 500 E-mini, with a 4-point upward move and a 2-point downward move.

3. Calculate position size (number of contracts)

Use this formula:

$$Number\ of\ contracts = \frac{Risk\ per\ trade}{Risk\ per\ contract}$$

Using the previous example:

Risk per trade = $500

Risk per contract = $100 → 500 / 100 = **5 contracts**

You should trade 5 contracts to stay within your risk limits.

9.4 HOW TO CALCULATE VOLATILITY BASED STOP-LOSSES

To set stop-loss levels based on the market volatility, we use the ATR (Average True Range), a volatility indicator. The ATR 14 measures the average price range over the last 14 candles.

9.4.1 STEPS TO CALCULATE A STOP-LOSS USING ATR14.

1. Find the ATR 14 value

- Find the ATR 14 of the asset for your selected timeframe.
- If the ATR 14 value is 2.5, it means the stock moves $2.50 on average per candle in your timeframe.

2. Decide your ATR multiplier

- A common approach is to take a multiplier between 1.5 and 2, depending on volatility and risk tolerance.
- If you use a tighter stop: go for 1.5 x ATR 14 (suitable for low-volatility assets).
- If you use a wider stop: go for 2 x ATR 14 (suitable for highly volatile assets).

3. Calculate the stop-loss level

- For long trades:

$$Stop\text{-}loss = Entry\ Price - (ATR14 \times Multiplier)$$

- For short trades:

$$Stop\text{-}loss = Entry\ Price + (ATR14 \times Multiplier)$$

Example:

Entry Price = $100

ATR14 = $2.50

Multiplier = 2

<u>Option 1: Long Trade</u>

Calculate the price at which you set your stop-loss:

$$100 - (2.5 \times 2) = 100 - 5 = \$95$$

→ Set a stop-loss at $95

9.5 A RELIABLE TRAILING STOP-LOSS STRATEGY

Trailing is adjusting the stop-loss level as the trade moves in your favor. Instead of setting a fixed stop-loss, a trailing stop follows the price at a set distance, locking in profits while allowing the trade to continue if the trend persists, even if small fluctuations happen.

There are many ways to trail a stop-loss, but I'll show you one of the most reliable and profitable methods, especially when trading in the stock or futures markets.

My recommended trailing strategy is suitable for the scenario in which you use three different target prices and works like this:

- Move your stop-loss to the entry point once target price 1 is reached.
- Move your stop-loss to Target Price 1 once target price 2 is reached.
- After price reaches the 2nd target price, only adjust your stop-loss when a strong candle appears, place the stop one tick below that candle.

Regardless of your trailing strategy, always keep these fundamental rules in mind:

- After achieving the 1st target price, move your stop-loss to break even and trail.
- Never let a winning trade turn into a losing one.

DO NOT MOVE YOUR STOP-LOSS UNTIL THE FIRST TARGET PRICE IS ACHIEVED.

9.6 FURTHER TRADING PARAMETERS

9.6.1 EXPECTANCY RATIO

The expectancy ratio measures how effective your trading strategy is by showing how much you can expect to make (or lose) per trade over time.

If you win 50% of the time, with an average profit of $200 and an average loss of $150, the expectancy ratio is:

$$Expectancy = (P\ x\ A) - [(1 - P)\ x\ L]$$

$$Expectancy = (0{,}5\ x\ 200) - [(1 - 0{,}5)\ x\ 150]$$

$$Expectancy = \$25\ per\ Trade$$

Where:

- P = Probability of a winning trade (win rate, in decimal form). A win rate of 50% means P=0,5.
- A = Average win (in dollars or R multiples)
- L = Average loss (in dollars or R multiples)

A positive expectancy indicates a profitable strategy.

Even if P is less than 50%, by aiming for a higher RR, you can develop profitable strategies, as long as the expectancy is positive.

9.6.2 MAXIMAL DRAWDOWN

The maximal drawdown (MDD) represents the maximum percentage decline from a peak to a trough in a trading account before a new peak is reached. If an account grows from $10,000 to $15,000 but then drops to $12,000 before recovering, the drawdown is:

$15,000 - $12,000 = $3,000

Lower drawdowns indicate better risk management.

9.6.3 Winning rate

The winning rate is the percentage of successful trades relative to total trades. For example, if you execute 100 trades and win 60, the win rate is 60%. A high win rate is desirable but should be analyzed alongside risk-reward ratios for overall profitability.

9.6.4 Bernoulli distribution

The Bernoulli calculation is used in probability-based trading models to estimate the likelihood of a sequence of wins or losses. It models a single trial with only two possible outcomes:

1 (success) or 0 (failure)

It's defined by a single parameter:

$$p = \text{Probability of success}$$

$$\text{and probability of failure} = 1-p$$

Let's say the win rate of a trading strategy is **60%**

➔ P (win) = 0.6 (probability of a winning trade)

If a trader has a 60% win probability, the likelihood of two consecutive wins is 36%. This helps in managing risk and expectations over multiple trades.

$$P\ (\text{two wins}) = p \times p = 0{,}36\ (36\%)$$

10 EXECUTION

To execute your transactions efficiently you can use different types of orders. The three primary order types are market orders, stop orders, and limit orders, each serving a distinct purpose.

A **market order** is an order to buy or sell a security immediately at the best available price. This type of order guarantees execution but does not guarantee the price, making it ideal when speed is more important than price precision. Market orders are commonly used in highly liquid markets where price fluctuations are minimal.

A **stop order** activates a market order when a specified price level (the stop price) is reached. There are two types: stop-loss orders and stop-buy orders. A stop-loss order is used to sell a security when its price drops to a certain level – helping to limit potential losses. Conversely, a stop-buy order is placed above the current market price and is used to enter a trade once price crosses that price level.

A **limit order** is an order to buy or sell a security at a specific price which ensures that you don't overpay.

A buy limit order is placed below the market price: only if price comes back to the buy limit order price, the buy market order will activate. While a sell limit order is set above the market price, only if price comes back to the sell limit order price, the buy market order will activate to secure a favorable sale.

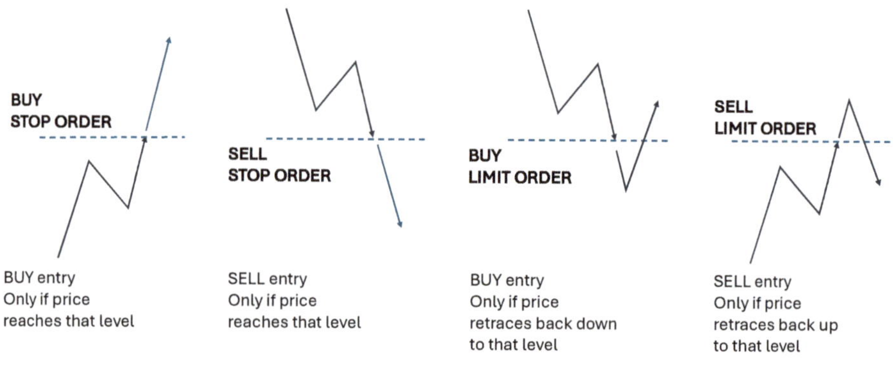

Limit orders provide price control but do not guarantee execution.

10.1 WHEN TO USE LIMIT ORDERS

You'll often come across good patterns and entry signals, where the distance between the entry point and the target price is though not enough to aim for the minimum risk-reward-ratio of 1, see example:

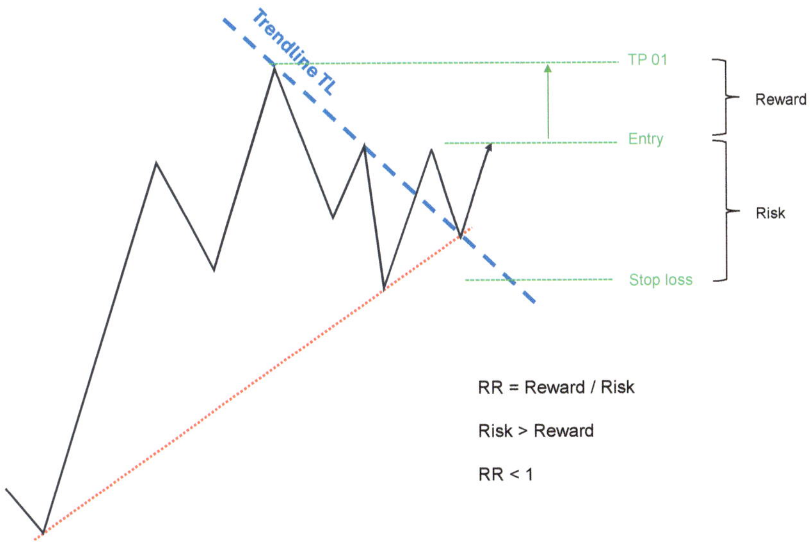

Example of a trade with a risk-reward ratio below 1:1 (RR<1): a valid pattern and entry signal, but an unfavorable entry due to proximity to the target price.

By using limit orders you can improve the risk-reward ratio of this type of trades. Why?

As markets move in waves, most of the time price is going to retrace a bit. With limit orders you can take advantage of this retracement and enter at a better price.

This approach ensures you enter the market at a favorable price rather than chasing price movements.

For short-term traders, such as scalpers or day traders, small price differences matter. A limit order helps maximize profit potential by ensuring execution at the most favorable price within a tight range.

10.2 HOW TO APPLY LIMIT ORDERS TO IMPROVE THE RISK-REWARD RATIO

When employing limit orders, the execution is done in 3-steps:

- **Step 1:** Wait for the theoretical trigger of the trade, which happens at the **trigger price**. In this example the trigger is the neckline of a W pattern.

- **Step 2:** Place your limit order at a price, which ensures your desired risk-reward ratio. This price becomes your entry point, let us call it **entry price** (in the image below, we aim for a RR > 1).
  Keep in mind, at this stage, your limit order is already placed, but you have not yet entered the trade.

- **Step 3:** Wait for the price to reach your limit order. Once it does, you are in the trade.

As you can see, it is very important to understand the difference between the **trigger price** and the **entry price**:

The trigger price just confirms that market conditions are aligned with your strategy, whereas the entry price is the price at which you actually enter the trade.

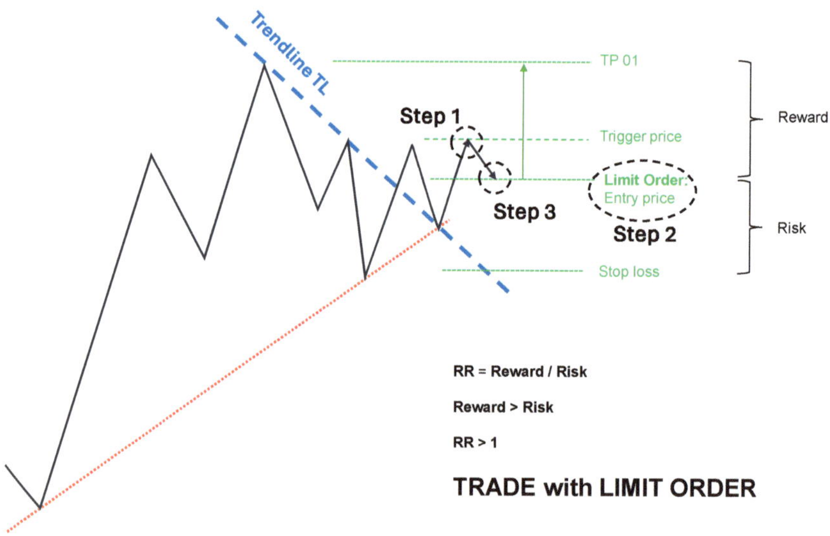

Example of a trade executed using a limit order to improve the risk-reward ratio of the trade.

The use of limit orders may appear and feel counterintuitive at first, yet it has consistently proven effective.

There will be occasions when the expected price retracement does not occur and your trade will not be executed, meaning you won't enter the position and you will miss a potential trade. However, accepting that imperfections is part of the process, it's far wiser to pass on a trade rather than risk entering a low-quality setup with a bad risk-reward ratio.

LIMIT ORDERS WILL IMPROVE THE RISK-REWARD RATIO OF YOUR TRADES

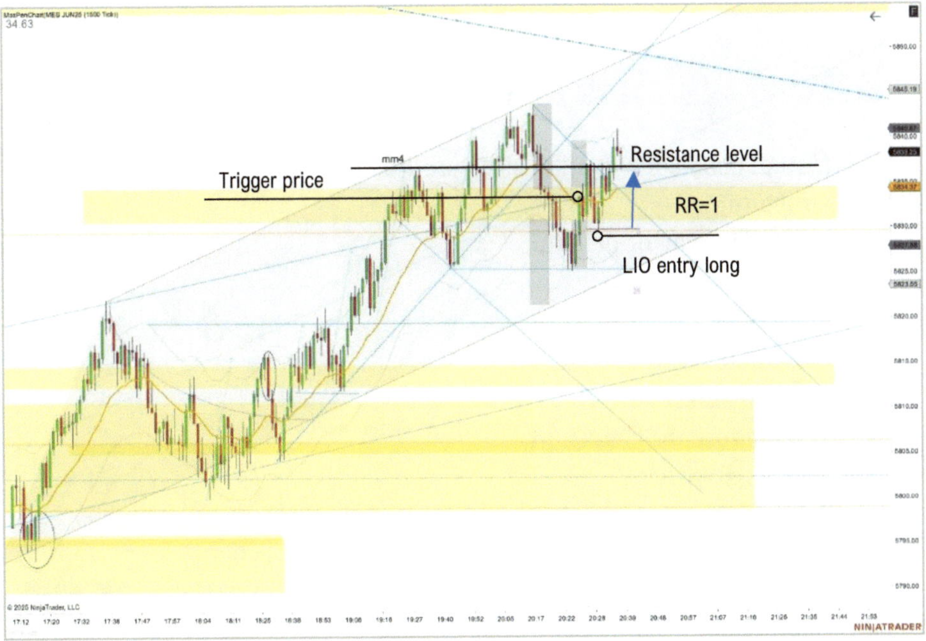

Example of limit order entry, to ensure a minimum RR (risk-reward ratio) of 1 for the trade.

11 TRADING JOURNAL

A trading journal is essential for improving your performance and building discipline. It allows you to track your trades, analyze patterns, and identify what's working, or what isn't. By reviewing past decisions, you will gain clarity, avoid repeating mistakes, and refine your strategy over time. It also keeps you accountable and emotionally grounded, especially during losing streaks or periods of overconfidence. A consistent journaling habit turns your experience into valuable insights.

I also recommend including **screenshots of your trades.** This helps you visually document the setup, market context, and your execution.

Your journal must also be **simple and easy to maintain,** if it's too complex or time-consuming, you're less likely to keep up with it, and its value will be diminished.

11.1 KEY PARAMETERS TO TRACK

- Market conditions: market structure (range, uptrend, downtrend or no structure).
- Setup, strategy or pattern.
- Entry signal.
- Entry price.
- ATR14 and Stop-loss size.
- Position size.
- Trade direction (long/short).
- Aimed risk-reward ratio.
- Target price according to your risk-reward ratio
- Real Outcome (PnL and RR). See Chapters 9.1 and 9.2.
- How do you feel? Track your emotions.
- Other notes.
- Stop-loss (has your SL been respected or modified?).

11.2 SAMPLE OF MY TRADING JOURNAL

TRADING JOURNAL

		Entry					Trade setup									Market Conditions						
x,d,s	Date	Time	Nr	Inst	L S	Vol	1,5 ATR ticks	used SL	TP1	TP2	TP3	Total	MAE	MFE	TP achieved	Market	Move	Retrace	Pattern	RR	li	EntrySignal
d	19.02	21:37	3	ES	L	1		10	-10	0		-10	8	0		Range_Up	LP_Strong_pro	1LP +	Failure	0,90		
d	19.02	21:54	4	ES	L	2		10	2	16		18	8	28		Range_Up	LP_Strong_pro	1LP +	Failure	0,90		
d	19.02	21:54	4	ES	L	2		10	2	16		18	8	28		Range_Up	LP_Strong_pro	1LP +	Failure	0,90		
d	19.02	10:44	5	ES	L	2		10	2	16		18	8	28		Range	LP_Strong	1LP +	Nested Failure	1,10		
d	26.02	06:50	1	NQ	S	1		72	60	0		60	2	80		Range_Dow	DLP_Normal_non	2LP	ailure + TL retest	1,50		Strong from EMA
d	26.02	08:49	2	NQ	S	1		72	60	0		60	0	120		Range_Dow	DLP_Normal_pro	2LP	NFailure + Space	1,30		Strong crossing EMA
d	26.02	09:17	3	NQ	S	1		72	72	0		72	20	80		Range_Dow	LP_normal_non	1LP	Failure	1,80		Pinbar

				Entry				Trade setup								Market Conditions							
x,d,s	Date	Time	Nr	Inst	L S	Vol	1,5 ATR ticks	used SL	TP1	TP2	TP3	Total	MAE	MFE	TP achieved	Market	Move	Retrace	Pattern	RR	li	EntrySignal	α
x	02.03	14:50	2	MES	L	2		30	69	137		206	0	164		Range	LP_Strong	1LP +	Nested Failure	3,0		Pinbar - Engulfing	
x	02.03	15:19	3	MES	L	2		30	6	6		12	6	45		Uptrend	Spike_Flag	Flag Flat	Failure+StrC	1,0			
x	02.03	15:45	4	MES	L	2		30	30	8		38	4	42		Range	LP_Strong	1LP +	Nested Failure	1,0		Strong above EMA	
x	02.03	16:04	4	MES	L	2		30	-30	-30		-60	75	3		Range	LP_Strong	1LP +	Nested Failure	2,0			
x	02.03	16:13	6	MES	L	2		30	33	15		48	12	34		Range	DLP_Normal_TL	1LP +	123 Reversal	1,5			
x	03.03	15:41	1	MES	L	2		30	10	10		20	18	19		Range	Up_Bias	2LP	Failure+TL	1,0			
x	04.03	14:22	1	MES	L	2		26	27	1		28	1	28		Uptrend	Spike_Channel	1LP +	TL retest + Failure	1,3			
s	04.03	14:22	2s	MES	L	2		26	26	1		27	0	28		Uptrend	Spike_Channel	1LP +	Trap	1,0			
s	04.03	14:40	3s	MES	L	2		26	26	1		27	0	28		Uptrend	Spike_Channel	1LP	Failure	0,9			
s	04.03	16:12	4s	MES	L	2		24	24	60		84	0	80		Range	Up_Bias	2LP +	NF+TL	2,5			
x	04.03	20:00	1	MNQ	L	2		35	35	1		36	0	35		Range	Up_Bias	2LP	NF+TL	1,0		Pinbar - Engulfing	
x	04.03	20:00	2	MNQ	S	2		35	-20	-20		-40	35	8		Range	Up_Bias	2LP	NF+TL	1,0		Normal crossing EMA	
x	04.03	20:41	3	MNQ	L	2		35	-35	-35		-70				Range	Up_Bias	1LP	Failure	0,0		Normal crossing EMA	
x	04.03	20:55	4	MNQ	S	2		35	-35	-35		-70				Range	Up_Bias	2LP	No	0,0		Strong from EMA	
x	04.03	21:00	5	MNQ	S	2		35	5	5		10				Range	Up_Bias	2LP	NF	0,0		Strong from EMA	

Example of "Analysis of losing trades":

			Market Conditions								Comments					
x,d,s	Date	Time	Market	Move	Retrace	Pattern	RR	li	EntrySignal	α	Pros	Cons / Risks	To Improve	Sample	PnL #	MFE #
s	11.03	10:05	Range	Down_Bias	1LP +	NF+Pb	0,6	x	Strong from EMA		if Executed --> LIO as to close to Range Border	Too close to Range Border	**Dont take trades at Range Border !!!** Trades in Range or close to Range: See MMs, HCH forming,TLs, TP a bit before			
s	11.03	10:50	Range	Down_Bias	1LP +	Trap	1,3		Engulfing		Trap at 1st deviation = Crown Reversal = Signal at pefect position of HCH forming		Dont take trades at Range Border !!! Trades in Range or close to Range: See MMs, HCH forming,TLs, TP a bit before			
s	11.03	10:50	Range	Down_Bias	1LP +	Pullback Shadow	0,7		Engulfing			at border Range --- inside the Range	Dont take trades at Range Border !!! Trades in Range or close to Range: See MMs, HCH forming,TLs, TP a bit before			
x	16.03		Uptrend	Spike_Channel	2LP +	Failure+StrC					123 Reversal up Triangle formation	Huge Spike Down - - In the middle of Trangle, indeicision area	Triangle, wait for Major RS level, bottom part of Triangle Not Waited for major RS level			
x	16.03		Uptrend	Spike_Channel	2LP +	Failure+StrC					124 Reversal up Triangle formation	Huge Spike Down - - In the middle of Trangle, indeicision area	Impulsive trade far from EMA !!!! In Mid of Triangle Not Waited for major RS level			
x	16.03		Range	Up_Bias	Flag Flat	Strength					Trap down could not move price further down	Above Triangle. Wait for Retest of Triangle	No Strength from Huge Triangle and on top of Uptrend.wait for Retest of Triangle.			
x	16.03		Uptrend	Spike_Channel	2LP +	Failure						Very strong move down. Wait for nested failure	Entry too late. Underbelly too close. RR bad			
x	16.03		Range	Down_Bias	1LP +	Failure	0,4				Exited sooner as soo as I realized entry is wrong	Long right at Range Border in Downtrend - -	Strong move down: Trap . Wait for proper leg!!!			
x	16.03		Uptrend	Spike_Channel	2LP +	Failure						Choppy area/ Mini Range: no	Strong Downtrend. Long only if clear 123			
x	16.03		Downtrend	Spike_Range		Failure						Long in the middle of Triangle (Range) - - -	Wait for second leg off EMA21 for 123 reversal. 1 strong leg is not enough NO LONGS in DOWNTREND !!!			
x	16.03		Downtrend	Spike_Range		Failure+StrC							NO LONGS in DOWNTREND !!!			
s	19.03	08:30	Uptrend	SdeepChannel	1LP	Pullback	2,0									
s	19.03	08:30	Uptrend	SdeepChannel	1LP	Pullback	1,2									
x	19.03	08:30	Uptrend	SdeepChannel		Strength	1,3									
s	19.03	09:00	Uptrend	SdeepChannel	1LP +	Failure	1,3				W very irregular. Delta red strong before failure					
s	19.03	09:00	Uptrend	SdeepChannel	1LP +	NF	1,1				Bottom part of triangle, enough RR					

12 PREPARATION OF A TRADING SESSION

12.1 CHECKLIST

1. Check if there are major news, which could generate an increase in volatility.
2. Find out when major news are scheduled to be released, and stay out of the market during that time. Econoday.com is a good platform for this purpose. Set an alarm to avoid those moments.
3. Check the maximal volatility during that day: just take a look at ATR14 and use it to define your stop-losses as explained in Chapter 9.4.1.
4. Define a maximal loss per trade, based on your account size. Risking 1% of your account per trade is common practice. Maintain a consistent risk percentage across all trades, and only increase risk if you have clearly defined in advance the conditions under which it is justified.
5. Prepare a trading journal, a digital spread sheet, where you can easily register your trades.
6. Visualize what you expect to happen on the chart to pull the trigger.
7. Be aware of the best times during the day to trade. If the market is too slow, it's better to wait rather than react impulsively just for the sake of being active. Trading is like fishing or hunting, you only pull the trigger when it makes sense.
8. Define a maximum number of trades for your trading day.
9. Define your 'NO WAY' trade list. These are situations where you should avoid putting your money at risk.
10. Define the timeframe in which you want to trade.
11. Check on a higher timeframe to see the overall context and the market structure.
12. Do the necessary technical analysis on advance:
    1. Find out the type of market: range-bound, trending or choppy.
    2. Define good entry areas on your chart: buy low, sell high!

3. Wait for price to return to ideal entry zones. The market will retrace at some point, be patient.
4. Look for an entry signal.
5. Check if there is enough space between your entry point and the most probable target price.
6. Is price moving toward an area of attraction? Where is it most likely to go? Where is the magnet?

13. Select the strategies you want to use. Less is more.

14. Analyze your emotions before trading, are you angry, anxious, in a hurry…

15. Make sure you have a concentrated atmosphere.

16. Be mentally prepared for a loss.

17. How many losses do you want to accept today?

18. According to my experience it is also good to set a maximal profit for a day. Once you reach it, stop trading and do something different!

19. More than 3 losses in a row are a warning sign. It is time to make a break an analyze. Do a post-mortem analysis.

20. Maintain your charts clean and understandable.

21. Don't doubt to place a trade as soon as all ingredients appear.

22. Don't move your stop-loss.

23. Wait for price to reach the first target price. From there on you can trail your stop-loss.

24. Never forget…

EVEN THE BEST-LOOKING TRADES CAN AND WILL FAIL AT SOME POINT…

YOU CAN NEVER KNOW WHEN THIS MOMENT COMES… BE PROTECTED AND USE ALWAYS A STOP-LOSS.

13 COMMON ERRORS

Throughout my trading career, I've meticulously documented a wide range of unique experiences and the invaluable lessons I've learned along the way.

Often, these lessons involve simple yet crucial concepts that can easily be overlooked.

In this chapter I want to share a list of recommendations and reflections that had a significant impact on the outcome of my trading journey.

13.1 THE FATAL EFFECT OF A LONG STREAK OF WINNING TRADES: OVERCONFINDENCE

Do you know the feeling of getting used to high-probability winning strategies?

They may give you the illusion of being able to predict the future. If you have experienced this feeling at some point, please read the following text carefully and reflect:

> *"After a long streak of winning trades, I started to believe that I had it all figured out. I thought I was a professional and could control the market. As my wins accumulated, I became more relaxed, thinking I could generate money quickly and effortlessly. I began fantasizing about what I could do with my profits, planning trips, buying gifts for my family, and making promises I couldn't wait to fulfill.*
>
> *At this point, my emotions became deeply tied to my trading results, and my expectations soared far beyond realistic levels. I started cutting corners, becoming careless with my stop-losses, convinced that the market would always move in my favor.*
>
> *But with that carelessness came a dangerous increase in risk. I didn't realize it then, but the risk of losing a significant portion of my account without limiting my losses was growing exponentially.*
>
> *Then, the market suddenly turned against me. My high-probability strategies, which had worked so well before, failed for the first time. And though I felt a protective mechanism tried to kick in, an attempt to shield myself from the harsh reality, I refused to accept what was happening.*

Emotion took over, and rational thinking shut down. Hope became my guiding force. Instead of cutting my losses and moving on, I held on, waiting for the market to recover. But the market didn't recover. It continued to move against me for far longer than I had expected.

In a desperate attempt to turn things around, I doubled down, adding to my positions and increasing my risk, even though I had no solid reasoning for doing so. I just wanted to be right. My ego wouldn't let me admit that I was wrong.

I held onto those losing trades for far too long. That misplaced conviction triggered a complete meltdown. Revenge trading took hold, and I spiralled out of control. In the end, I lost everything, my account wiped out, all because I ignored the fundamental principles of risk management and let my emotions dictate my actions".

DON'T LET A MELTDOWN HAPPEN TO YOU

13.2 NEVER CONVERT A SHORT-TERM TRADE IN A LONG-TERM INVESTMENT: THE EMOTIONAL ATTACHMENT

A common phenomenon in trading occurs when traders transform a short-term trade into long-term investment due to emotional attachment, fear, or denial.

This scenario often happens when a trader's position starts moving against them, and instead of sticking to their original plan and cutting losses, they hold onto the position or even add more, thinking it will eventually recover. Such behavior is especially dangerous because it breaks the most important risk management principles.

One of the primary triggers for this shift is the confirmation bias. Traders may become emotionally invested in a position, convincing themselves that the market will turn around in their favor.

THEY OFTEN BEGIN SEARCHING FOR REASONS TO JUSTIFY THEIR DECISION

...even if it contradicts their original plan or strategy. This process of self-justification can take various forms:

One common behavior is **looking for news that supports their decision**, even if the information is not directly relevant or significant. For instance, they may latch onto a minor positive update about the company, hoping it will reverse the trend, despite the overall market sentiment suggesting otherwise.

Another form of self-justification is blaming others: market analysts, economic conditions, or even other traders for the downturn, arguing that the market is simply misunderstanding the asset's value.

Traders might fail to recognize that their decision to hold on is driven by emotional attachment, not objective analysis.

In some cases, traders fall into denial, convincing themselves that the market will turn around soon, despite evidence to the contrary.

SELF-JUSTIFICATION IS FOCUSING ON SMALL, HOPEFUL SIGNALS AND IGNORE THE BROADER CONTEXT, REFUSING TO ACCEPT THE REALITY OF BEING WRONG

Traders may also reinterpret their losses, telling themselves that the asset is temporarily undervalued and that it will eventually recover, rationalizing that they are merely "holding through the dip."

This leads to averaging down, where traders buy more shares at a lower price, believing they're getting a better deal.

While this might work sometimes, it also increases their exposure and risk, making it harder to recover if the position continues to decline.

An unexpected event, such as news about a company's fraud or an economic crisis, can trigger an abrupt price movement. If traders still hold their position, they risk losing a significant portion of their capital. The worst part is that emotions take over, and traders fall into the trap of hope, waiting for a recovery rather than accepting the reality of the situation.

Without discipline and a clear plan, which has to be respected every single day, traders are more likely to turn their trades into gambling, and ultimately lose everything.

13.3 THE PRODUCTIVITY TRAP IN TRADING

A common phenomenon among novice traders is the **feeling that they must be constantly active in the market** and be productive, even if there's no clear opportunity. This sense of urgency leads them to force trades when there's no valid setup, simply because they feel the need to be doing something.

In such cases, they often chase small market movements or jump into trades based on impulses or market noise. Instead of patiently waiting for a proper setup that aligns with their strategy, they make decisions based on fear of missing out (FOMO) or the desire to "get in" before everyone else. This behavior frequently results in overtrading, taking positions in the market even though the conditions are not ideal.

Forced trades tend to lack proper risk management and are driven by emotional impulses for action rather than strategic thinking. The outcome is often unnecessary losses and frustration.

> ***THE CORE IS SIMPLE: TRADING FOR THE SAKE OF BEING ACTIVE IS A FAST TRACK TO LOSING MONEY***

Successful trading is not about constant action, it's about waiting for quality opportunities and executing them with discipline.

> ***WAIT FOR QUALITY OPPORTUNITIES, DON'T FORCE TRADES***

Excessive trading not only increases emotional stress and risk exposure but also **racks up significant trading fees**. Each unnecessary trade adds to transaction costs, which can quietly eat away at your profits over time. Even small fees accumulate quickly, turning potentially winning strategies into losing ones through sheer volume of trades.

14 COMPONENTS OF A GOOD TRADE

Taking care of every detail of a quality trade can boost your chances of being successful in trading. Pay close attention to these key elements. They may seem obvious, but they are fundamental, and often the difference between consistent success and repeated failure.

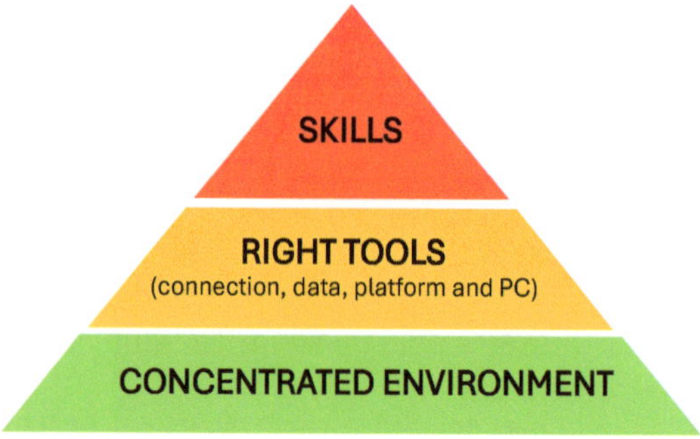

- **Concentrated working environment:**
    - **Work in a concentrated environment**
      Not at the beach or in a cafe or in a train. During trading, you must stay focus and not depend on external factors. **Don't let yourself be influenced by flashy trading adds showing people trading from beach bars.**

- **Right Tools and Data:**
    - **Good internet connection.**
      Professional traders always have a back-up internet connection to be able to close a trade if the main internet connection fails. An internet connection via your mobile phone as a back-up is enough at the beginning.
    - **Stable trading platform.**
      Some platforms crash when the market is moving the most. Platforms like "Trader Workstation", "TC2000" or "Ninja Trader" have proven to be stable.
    - **Stable computer.**
      Check the minimum specifications required to run your trading platform. It is advisable to have some additional computing power

beyond the minimum requirements to ensure stability and avoid performance issues during fast market conditions.

  - **Stable market data provider.**
    Real-time market data is essential for making informed decisions. Traders rely on data for price movements, volume, order flow, and news updates. Delayed or inaccurate data can lead to missed opportunities, poor trade execution, or unexpected losses.
    A reliable market data provider ensures low-latency, real-time quotes, allowing you to react quickly to changing market conditions.

- **Skills:**
  - Do you have the knowledge to successfully participate in the market?
  - Do you have a working strategy?
  - Have you applied this strategy in a demo account?
  - Have you applied this strategy in real account with a small size?
  - Have you developed the ability to scale your trading size without getting emotional?
  - Can you accept that your stop-loss can get hit, even when a trade and strategy look perfect?

- **Psychological strength:**
  - Patience.
  - Discipline.
  - Controlling emotions, such as fear and greed.
  - Be realistic and manage your expectations.

MASTERING THE RIGHT EXECUTION

- **Understanding the market structure.**
  How is price moving? Where does price want to go?

- **Predefining the right places to buy or sell.**
  What is a low price and what is high?
  Use professional technical analysis.

- **Waiting for the right entries.**
  Identify high quality patterns and entry signals. And be patience and discipline. Avoid emotional or impulsive entries.

- **Recognizing the right exits.**
  Exiting a trade at the right time is just as important as the entry. Whether locking in profits or cutting losses, a well-planned exit strategy prevents unnecessary risks. Even losing trades, when exited correctly, protect capital and allow you to recover in future opportunities.

15 PSYCHOLOGY

It is important to know the different psychological challenges and emotions that you will encounter while trading. By being aware of them, you will be able to anticipate when it is time to pause, reflect, stop trading or take a longer break from the markets.

15.1 MELTDOWN EFFECT

The meltdown behavior of a trader refers to the psychological and **emotional breakdown** that occurs when a trader experiences significant stress, frustration, or panic, often after a series of losing trades.

This emotional collapse can lead to poor decision-making, impulsive actions, and **irrational behavior** that ultimately worsens the situation. It's similar to a "mental crash," where you lose control over your emotions and decision-making process.

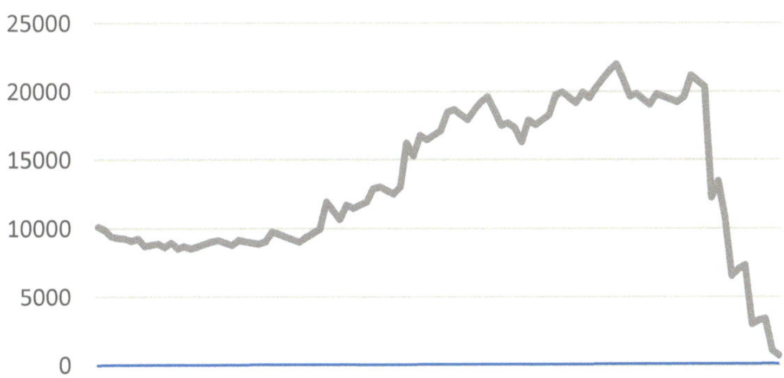

Example of a trading account before and after the melt-down effect

15.1.1 KEY CHARACTERISTICS OF A TRADER'S MELTDOWN BEHAVIOR

15.1.1.1 Emotional overreaction

Traders experiencing a meltdown often overreact emotionally to market movements, leading to impulsive decisions. For instance, selling a position at the worst possible moment because they fear further losses, or they may chase after a trade in a desperate attempt to recover previous losses.

Emotions like fear, greed, frustration, and hopelessness can cloud your judgment, preventing you from thinking logically or from following your trading plan.

15.1.1.2 Chasing losses - Revenge trading

One of the most common signs of a trader's meltdown is revenge trading, a compulsive attempt to recover losses by making increasingly larger or riskier trades.

Revenge trading often leads to even bigger losses, as it is driven by emotional impulse rather than rational analysis.

15.1.1.3 Breaking trading rules

A trader in meltdown mode may completely disregard their trading rules and often lose the ability to make objective and rational decisions.

For example:

- They may ignore their stop-loss orders or place them too tightly in an effort to avoid or minimize losses, without adequately evaluating the prevailing market conditions.
- They might abandon their **risk-to-reward ratios** and enter trades without considering whether the potential reward justifies the risk.
- They may fail to follow a **trading plan**, jumping from one strategy to another without clear logic or consistency.
- **They begin to hope.**

15.1.1.4 Overtrading

In an attempt to "make up for lost ground," it is common to start overtrading, taking too many positions or using excessive leverage. This behavior often follows a series of losses or a sharp drawdown.

Overtrading significantly increases the likelihood of poor decision-making, as the pressure to recover losses can create a feeling of needing to trade every opportunity, further intensifying emotional stress.

15.1.1.5 Loss of confidence and self-doubt

A trader going through a meltdown may experience a **loss of confidence** in their ability to succeed, especially if losses keep mounting. Self-doubt creeps in, leading to feelings of **incompetence** or **failure**.

This loss of self-confidence can cause them to second-guess every decision or avoid making trades altogether, creating a sense of paralysis or indecision.

15.1.1.6 Rationalization and denial

In some cases, traders might **rationalize** their mistakes, trying to convince themselves that they didn't make a bad decision or that the market will turn in their favor. This denial can prevent them from acknowledging their errors and adjusting their approach.

This behavior is often a defence mechanism, helping the trader avoid confronting the reality of their losses.

15.1.1.7 Betting everything on one trade

After a string of losses, there is often a tendency to take on excessive risk, such as abandoning proper risk management or betting everything on a single trade in an attempt to recover quickly.

These high-risk, high-reward trades are often emotionally motivated and are more likely to result in catastrophic losses.

15.1.1.8 Avoiding the market (Shutdown)

A severe loss or a prolonged run of poor trades can lead to a mental shutdown. In this state, stepping away from the market altogether, sometimes for an extended period, can feel like the only option, driven by emotional exhaustion or a sense of defeat.

This avoidance can also lead to feelings of **guilt** or **shame**, which further impairs their ability to move forward and learn from their mistakes.

15.1.1.9 Overemphasis on Short-Term Outcomes

During a meltdown phase, attention often shifts toward short-term results rather than long-term consistency and profitability. The urge for immediate gratification, whether through quick wins or rapid loss recovery, can cloud judgment and lead to decisions that are detrimental in the long run.

15.2 OVERCONFIDENCE

Overconfidence in trading refers to a cognitive bias where traders believe they have more knowledge, skill, or control over the market than they actually do. This overestimation of one's abilities can lead to excessive risk-taking, poor decision-making, and ultimately, significant losses. It's a common psychological trap that many traders fall into, often after experiencing some success or when they rely too heavily on their own analysis without considering the full range of potential market outcomes.

Traders with overconfidence may feel compelled to trade frequently, believing that they can consistently beat the market. This leads to excessive trading activity, often resulting in unnecessary transaction costs and increased exposure to risk.

This short-term focus often causes traders to jump in and out of positions too frequently, reducing their chances of success. Overtrading can also be driven by the belief that past successes will continue, even if the market environment has changed.

Overconfident traders might take on disproportionately large positions relative to their account size.

They may only seek information that confirms their existing beliefs or trade decisions, dismissing contrary evidence. This selective attention reinforces their overconfidence and can lead to faulty decision-making, as they ignore red flags or alternative viewpoints that might suggest caution.

15.3 THE ROLE OF ENDORPHINS IN OVERTRADING

Endorphins are chemicals produced by the brain that are often referred to as "feel-good" hormones. They are released during activities like exercise, eating, and even trading, particularly when you experience positive emotions or rewards from your actions.

Overtrading and endorphins are connected in a way that explains why some traders may find themselves engaged in excessive trading despite the risks involved. Understanding this mechanism is key to manage your reactions.

In the context of overtrading, endorphins play a critical role in the psychology behind the behavior. Here's how:

- **The reward system**: Trading can trigger the release of endorphins because successful trades or even the excitement of entering a new trade can create a sense of pleasure or euphoria. When traders experience a winning trade or anticipate potential gains, their brain associates trading with a "reward," and endorphins are released. This gives traders a sense of excitement, pleasure, or satisfaction, which is a powerful motivator.
- **Chasing the high**: Similar to addictive behaviors, traders who get a "rush" from a successful trade may seek to replicate the feeling, leading them to take excessive risks or trade more often. The feeling of winning, whether it's from profit or the excitement of the market, can trigger a cycle where traders overtrade to experience that endorphin release again and again. This is comparable to how people might overeat, overdrink, or engage in other addictive behaviors to chase a "high."

Overtrading can also be driven by a desire to avoid the negative feelings associated with losses.

While the release of endorphins in response to winning trades can feel rewarding, it can create a **dangerous feedback loop** in traders. Here's why:

- **Addiction to the Rush**: Just like in gambling or other forms of addiction, the pursuit of the endorphin-driven rush can cause traders to overestimate their abilities, ignore risk management, and take excessive risks. Over time, this can lead to significant losses as traders chase that feeling of excitement or satisfaction, often at the cost of their long-term financial stability.

- **Emotional Rollercoaster**: Overtrading can lead to emotional volatility, riding high with wins and feeling crushed with losses. The ebb and flow of emotions can be amplified by the fluctuating release of endorphins, making it difficult to make rational, objective decisions.
- **Desensitization to Risk**: As traders become accustomed to the endorphin rush of successful trades, **they may become desensitized to the risks involved in their actions**. Over time, they might take larger and larger risks to try and get that same level of excitement or reward, gradually escalating the danger they face in the market.
- **Pain masking:** Endorphins can also mask the psychological pain of market stress.

15.3.1 *HOW TO COMBAT THE ENDORPHIN RUSH*

Set clear rules and limits

Establishing a set of trading rules and limits (e.g., maximum trades per day, risk per trade, or daily profit/loss targets) can help mitigate impulsive trading driven by emotional highs or lows.

Take breaks

Taking conscious breaks away from trading helps reset emotional triggers and reduce the compulsive desire to constantly monitor the markets or make trades. It also recharges your energy and rebalances your emotional and hormonal state.

Practice mindfulness and self-awareness

Being aware of your emotional state before and during trading can help you identify when you're acting impulsively or seeking the "rush" of a trade. Mindfulness techniques can help you stay grounded and avoid making decisions based on emotions rather than logic or strategy.

TAKE BREAKS, EVEN IF YOUR RESULTS ARE SATISFACTORY

15.3.1.1 Focus on long-term goals

Focusing on long-term profitability and setting realistic trading goals can reduce the urge to make quick, high-risk trades for immediate gratification. Building discipline and sticking to a trading plan can help break the cycle of chasing the endorphin rush.

15.4 LOSS AVERSION. INABILITY TO ACCEPT LOSSES

According to behavioral economics, people tend to feel the pain of losses more acutely than the pleasure of gains. In this context, a trader may become fixated and even obsessed on avoiding the emotional discomfort of accepting a loss (loss aversion), causing them to hold onto a trade longer than they should.

PEOPLE TEND TO FEEL THE PAIN OF LOSSES MORE ACUTELY THAN THE PLEASURE OF GAINS.

When traders experience a loss, they often feel anxious, frustrated, or upset. In an attempt to counter these emotions, they may make impulsive trades, hoping for a quick win to recover losses or boost their mood. Alternatively, they might hold on to losing positions too long, failing to recognize when it would be wiser to exit and minimize further damage.

This behaviour can be linked to the brain's reward system, where traders seek another win to release endorphins and offset the negative feelings from a loss.

To manage the bias of perceiving losses as more painful than gains, I recommend the following approach:

- Consider each trade as money that has already been spent, similar to an expense you may not recover. This mindset helps you accept potential losses before they occur.
- Remember that trading financial assets is no different from buying and selling physical goods, apply the same risk management principles.

You need to train yourself to view stop-losses as a protective tool that works in your favor, rather than a setback. While this may sound simple, it's a concept that many traders struggle to implement consistently over the long term. In fact, this mindset is often the key reason why many traders fail.

CONSIDER EACH TRADE AS MONEY THAT HAS ALREADY BEEN SPENT, SIMILAR TO AN EXPENSE YOU MAY NOT RECOVER

15.4.1 LOSSES ACCEPTANCE IN PHYSICAL GOODS TRADING

Losses are more easily accepted in physical goods trading compared to trading financial instruments due to several psychological and practical factors.

We can learn from this perspective.

First, physical goods are tangible, making their value more concrete and easier to assess. Traders often view losses in physical goods as part of a predictable transaction process. In contrast, financial instruments like stocks or currencies are intangible and subject to market volatility, which can feel more abstract and difficult to predict, leading to emotional responses and resistance to accepting losses.

Additionally, the **expectation of recovery** is often stronger in financial markets. Holding on to the hope of recouping losses quickly can cloud judgment and lead to impulsive decisions.

In physical goods trading, losses are generally seen as part of the business process, and risk is usually managed in advance through predictable pricing and demand.

Moreover, traders of financial instruments tend to develop an emotional attachment to their financial investments, making losses harder to accept. In physical goods, traders are usually more detached from individual transactions.

Example of loss acceptance with physical goods - concert tickets:

Imagine you buy 10 concert tickets for $100 each, intending to sell them for $120 each.
Risk: If you can't sell any tickets, your total loss is 10 × $100 = $1,000.
Reward: If you sell all tickets at your target price, your total profit is 10 × ($120 – $100) = $200.

Now, consider this: Would you buy 100 tickets instead of 10?

Probably not.

Why?

- If you fail to sell them, your loss increases to 100 × $100 = $10,000.
- Even though your potential profit increases by 10 times, you wouldn't be comfortable investing $10,000 upfront without having a high confidence in selling the tickets.

Applying this mindset to trading

Why should trading financial assets be any different? Before entering a trade, ask yourself:

- How much am I willing to risk upfront, just like a physical purchase?
- What is the maximum loss I am comfortable accepting?

By adopting this perspective, you can develop a disciplined and rational approach to trading, minimizing emotional decision-making and improving your overall performance.

15.5 PERSONAL ISSUES OR STRESS OUTSIDE OF TRADING

External stress factors, such as financial difficulties, health problems, or personal issues, can exacerbate emotional reactions while trading. Stress from life outside of trading can spill over into the trader's mindset, making them more likely to act impulsively or emotionally.

> ***IF YOU FEEL STRESS, DON'T TRADE***

15.6 THE "THIS TIME I HAVE TO BE RIGHT" BIAS

It is a psychological bias where traders feel a strong emotional need to prove that their previous predictions or decisions are correct, especially after experiencing a series of losses or setbacks.

They repeat over and over again their decision, looking for a confirmation at some point. They become more focused on being "right" than on rational analysis, risk management, or adapting to changing market conditions.

They usually have an excessive desire for validation. Admitting a loss, or being wrong is seen as a blow to their ego, so they fight harder to be right in order to preserve their sense of competence and self-esteem.

15.7 SELF-JUSTIFICATION

Traders may justify and rationalize their poor decisions or losses by thinking they are exceptions to the rule. They might blame the market or external factors for a loss rather than acknowledging that they ignored the risks or did not follow their own trading plan.

15.8 THE "THIS CAN NOT HAPPEN TO ME" BIAS

The "This can't happen to me" bias in trading refers to a psychological bias where traders believe that certain negative events or outcomes, such as significant losses, sudden market crashes, or mistakes, won't happen to them, despite the fact that these events are common in the market.

It's a form of cognitive bias or overconfidence, where traders think they are immune to the risks that affect others.

15.9 DON'T OVERLOOK THE GOOD WHILE SEARCHING FOR THE PERFECT

15.9.1 NOT FOR PERFECTIONISTS

Trading is not for perfectionists. While it may seem like achieving flawless trades is the goal, the reality is far different. In fact, perfectionism can be detrimental to a trader's success. Markets are inherently uncertain and unpredictable, and no one can consistently make perfect decisions. In fact, seeking perfection often leads to overanalysis, hesitation, and missed opportunities.

Perfectionists tend to obsess over every trade, wanting to execute the "perfect" entry and exit.

Successful traders focus on consistent profitability rather than perfection. They embrace small losses as part of the process and aim to manage risk effectively. The key is not to execute **perfect trades but to follow a well-defined strategy and adapt to changing market conditions. Mistakes are inevitable**, but they offer valuable lessons that can improve your trading over time.

DEALING WITH IMPERFECTION IS PART OF THE GAME

15.9.2 ANALYSIS PARALISIS

When traders become too focused on finding the **absolute best trade**, they might overanalyze charts, news, or data, which can prevent them from making any trade at all. This is a common result of trying to find the “better” trade. They may believe that **waiting** for the "best" moment is better than acting on the “good” opportunity that’s already available.

This mindset can lead to paralysis by analysis, where they overthink each decision instead of acting decisively. In trading, waiting for the ideal setup can result in lost profits or unnecessary losses, as markets don’t always behave according to our expectations.

While aiming for perfection is understandable, the reality is that perfect trades are rare and can often lead to missed opportunities or analysis paralysis (spending too much time analyzing and not taking action).

15.9.3 Set realistic expectations

Accept that not every trade will be a home run. There will always be opportunities that are "good enough" but not perfect. Set **realistic expectations about the return you expect from your trades** and be willing to take those opportunities when they arise.

Be cautious of increasing your profit expectations after a winning streak, since they can lead to unrealistic assumptions. It's essential to stay adaptable and align with the market's current conditions, avoiding the trap of constantly aiming for unrealistic results.

15.10 TO BE IN A HURRY

A lack of patience or time can result in poor entries and missed opportunities that would have been more favorable with a disciplined approach.

Rushed traders may fail to wait for the ideal trading setup, entering trades prematurely or outside of their preferred risk/reward parameters. They might make quick decisions without taking the time to thoroughly analyze the market or their trade setups. This can lead to taking positions driven by emotions or intuition, instead of adhering to a clear, established strategy.

Skipping the confirmation of a technical indicator, condition or news release just to be involved in a trade can backfire.

Just a short personal story, that happened to me.

> *"My worst trade happened just an hour before I went on holiday with my family. After packing all the suitcases, I had 30 minutes left, which I unfortunately spent trading stock options. It started off well, and I left two big trades open, thinking I could close them later in the week. I got into the car heading to our holiday destination, not monitoring the trades, confident that everything would be fine. Had I kept an eye on those trades instead of leaving them unattended, the outcome could have been very different. Instead, within just three days, stock prices dropped sharply and my options became almost worthless, resulting in a complete loss of my investment."*

Don't enter a trade if you don't have the patience or time to execute it properly

15.11 TRADING WILL CHALLENGE YOU AT SOME POINT

At some point in every trader's journey, the markets will challenge you in ways that are difficult to anticipate. Trading isn't just about understanding technical charts or making quick decisions, it's about **emotional resilience** and the ability to adapt to constant changes. You will face losses, frustrating periods of low performance, and moments where even the best strategies seem to fail. These are the times that truly test your character as a trader.

To recover from setbacks, manage your emotions and develop a high frustration tolerance.

The real challenge comes when you're forced to confront your own fears, doubts, and overconfidence. Emotions like fear, greed, and frustration can cloud your judgment, pushing you to make impulsive decisions that go against your strategy and real interests.

Market conditions will change unexpectedly, and sometimes even the best analysis won't guarantee success.

It's during these tough times that the mental game becomes more important than the technical one

Trading will challenge your ability to stick to your plan, to manage risk, and to stay disciplined when emotions are high. The key is to learn from these challenges, not be defeated by them. Every setback offers an opportunity to grow, refine your approach, and build the emotional fortitude needed for long-term success. Embrace the challenge, as it is an essential part of becoming a skilled and successful trader.

AIMING FOR CONSISTENCY RATHER THAN PERFECTION IS THE PATH TO LONG-TERM SUCCESS

15.12 THE HARDEST PART IS TO ACCEPT A LOSING STREAK

One of the hardest challenges in trading is accepting a losing streak. After a series of successful trades, a sudden shift in the market can lead to consecutive losses, which can feel like a blow to your confidence. It's easy to get emotionally attached to the outcome of each trade, especially when losses accumulate, leading to frustration and self-doubt. However, it's crucial to remember that losing streaks are a natural part of trading.

The key to recovering is maintaining emotional discipline and sticking to your plan. First, **accept that losses are inevitable** and part of the journey. Instead of trying to force the market to work in your favor, take a step back and reevaluate your strategy. This allows you to spot any potential errors or areas for improvement.

During a losing streak, it's vital to manage your risk carefully. Avoid the temptation to overtrade or increase position sizes to compensate for losses. This often leads to even bigger losses. Instead, focus on consistent, small wins and ensure that your risk-reward ratio is favorable.

Lastly, take a break if needed. A clear mind is essential for making rational decisions. By reflecting on your trading and sticking to your principles, you can weather the storm and come back stronger. Resilience and adaptability are key to long-term recovery and success.

15.13 DETACHING THE VALUE OF THE MONEY YOU ARE TRADING WITH

When you're emotionally attached to the money in your trading account, it becomes difficult to make rational decisions. Fear of losing money or greed for making more can cloud your judgment, leading to impulsive actions, like overtrading, chasing losses, or ignoring stop-losses.

The key is to view trading as a process rather than focusing on the immediate monetary outcomes. Successful traders understand that profits and losses are just part of the journey. **They detach themselves from the emotional value of money and focus on the long-term strategy and consistency**.

One effective way to achieve this is by treating the trading capital as a business investment or using funds you can afford to lose. This mindset helps you avoid emotional attachment, making it easier to stick to your trading plan and risk management rules. It also allows you to make objective decisions without the pressure of needing a win right away.

By detaching from the emotional value of your capital, you can think more clearly, stay disciplined, and make better decisions, leading to more sustainable and long-term trading success.

Using RR units to evaluate your trades, helps detach from the monetary outcome by focusing on the risk-to-reward ratio instead of "dollar" amounts. This approach allows you to avoid the emotional attachment to financial results. See Chapter 9 "Risk Management."

15.14 BE PATIENT: IT TAKES TIME TO BE PROFITABLE

Becoming a profitable trader is not an overnight achievement. It takes time, patience, and a willingness to learn from both successes and failures.

In the beginning, trading can be very frustrating, especially when you compare yourself to more experienced traders, as you will often face losses and setbacks. However, it's important to understand that trading is a skill, and like any skill, it requires consistent practice and refinement.

Profitability in trading comes from developing a solid strategy, mastering risk management, and gaining a deep understanding of market behaviour and of yourself. During this journey, there will be times of uncertainty and mistakes. Over time, you'll learn to read market conditions, adjust your strategies, and build the emotional resilience needed to stick to your plan.

The key is staying disciplined and not rushing the process. **Profits accumulate over time through consistent, calculated decisions, not by seeking quick wins.** So, embrace the learning curve, focus on long-term growth, and accept that it takes time to truly become a consistently profitable trader.

15.15 GAINING CONFIDENCE WITH SMALL WINS

It's much more effective to focus on achieving many small wins rather than relying on an occasional large win.

Consistency is key in trading, and regular, smaller gains help to build long-term success. These small wins will accumulate over time, reducing risk and preventing the emotional rollercoaster that comes with chasing big, unpredictable profits. By focusing on steady, manageable gains, you can maintain discipline and stay in control.

It's the compound effect of these small wins that leads to consistent profitability, rather than relying on the luck of a single, large trade.

RELY ON THE COMPOUND EFFECT OF SMALL WINS

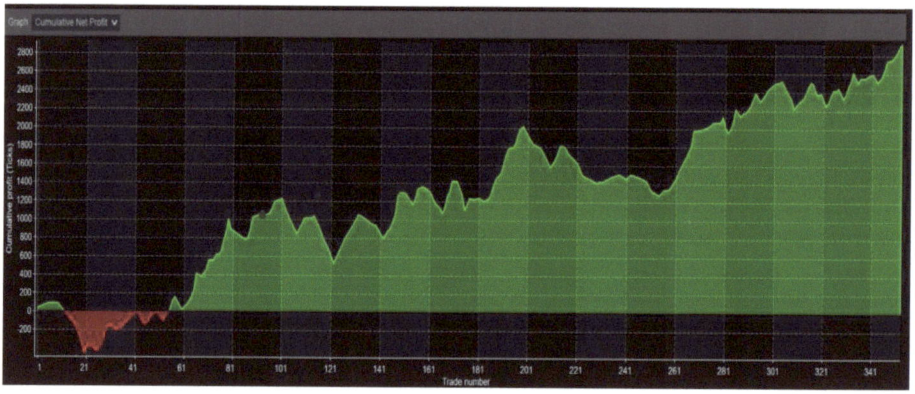

Example of a healthy trading account after more than 300 trades in the futures market.

15.16 SEPARATE TRADING ACTIVITIES FROM YOUR DAILY LIFE

Constantly checking trades or looking for new opportunities throughout the day could disrupt your focus, create unnecessary stress, and lead to impulsive decisions.

Trading at the beach or in holidays may sound appealing, but the truth is, it **will interfere with your life** at some point if you don't manage it in a proper way.

For this reason, it is important to separate trading activities from daily life and family time.

The highs and lows of trading can become addictive, making it hard to fully disconnect. When boundaries are not maintained, trading can affect concentration at work, strain personal relationships, and disrupt basic routines such as sleep and meals.

When you're distracted or anxious from constant updates, it will be hard for you to keep rational thinking and emotional discipline.

Avoid **using your smartphone** to monitor short-term trades. Instead try to set aside specific times during the day to review your trades and make decisions.

Try to **maintain your emotional balance** and create clear boundaries between trading and your personal life, this separation will allow you to reduce stress, avoid unnecessary distractions and make more objective decisions.

15.17 ACCOUNTABLITY PARTNER

An accountability partner can **help you stay disciplined and focused on your goals.** Trading can be an emotional rollercoaster, and it's easy to make impulsive decisions driven by fear, greed, or frustration.

Your accountability partner should be a trusted honest person, who helps you stay on track, questions decisions, ensures you're following your trading plan and **helps you maintain perspective during losing streaks or periods of doubt, offering encouragement and guidance.**

Regular check-ins and open discussions with your partner can foster self-reflection, helping you learn from mistakes, improve your decision-making over time, and stay accountable to your strategy, while also reminding you not to stray from your risk management rules.

Additionally, sharing your progress with an accountability partner can bring a sense of camaraderie and **reduce** the **isolation** often felt in trading.

15.18 ADDICTION IN DAY TRADING, THE HEALTHY APPROACH

15.18.1 WHY DAY TRADING CAN BE ADDICTIVE

Day trading can become addictive because of the excitement and potential for rapid profits. For some, executing trades and seeing immediate results activates the brain's reward system, much like gambling.

The constant anticipation of gains and the fear of missing out often push traders to make impulsive, emotional decisions. This emotional rollercoaster, paired with the allure of high returns, can become highly addictive.

Be aware of these psychological triggers and maintain a balanced approach to day trading. Only by recognizing the emotional drivers behind your actions will you be able to implement strategies to manage your emotions and avoid falling into the trap of addiction.

15.18.2 SIGNS OF DAY TRADING ADDICTION

While trading is a fascinating challenge, it's essential to recognize the signs of day trading addiction to protect both your financial stability and emotional well-being.

A key sign is an obsession with recovering lost money, which can lead to increased risk-taking and impulsive trades. This cycle of loss and the desperate drive to recover mirrors behaviors commonly seen in gambling addiction.

Another sign is the inability to stop trading, even after significant losses. Traders may feel an overwhelming urge to constantly check the markets, become anxious about their trades, and neglect other important areas of their lives.

Traders may also hide their activities or lie to friends and family about their losses.

If you recognize yourself when reading this chapter, it's important to take necessary steps to address the issue, such as setting strict limits, taking a meaningful break, or even seeking professional help, in order to regain control and maintain a healthier approach over time.

16 TRADING SKILLS: ANALOGY TO SPORTS

The analogy between sports and trading shows how the mental game, strategy, and resilience play a key role in both fields, ultimately driving success over time. In both, success is not only determined by raw talent or skill but also by the ability to stay focused, adapt to changing conditions, and manage pressure effectively. Apply the skills developed through sports to strengthen your trading performance.

To illustrate this parallel more clearly, let us take tennis as a reference. In tennis, players must stay patient, wait for the right moment to make a move, and recover from mistakes. Traders face similar challenges, as they must navigate unpredictable market conditions, make calculated decisions, and remain emotionally steady. Here are some important similarities:

- **Focus and mental discipline**

  Sustained focus and mental clarity are essential when every decision matters. Whether executing a precise shot or managing a position, success depends on blocking out distractions, acting decisively in the moment, and maintaining composure under pressure.

- **Adapting to changing conditions**

  Conditions are rarely static. Volatility shifts, new information emerges, and market structure evolves, demanding constant adjustment. Success depends on recognizing change early, responding decisively, and adapting to both to external factors and internal states, such as energy, focus, confidence and opponent's reactions, without emotional resistance.

- **Risk management**

  Every decision involves a balance between potential gain and potential loss. Success depends on accurately weighing opportunity against risk, knowing when to act decisively and when restraint is the better choice. Consistent performance emerges from disciplined evaluation rather than emotional impulse.

- **Strategy and tactics**

  A tennis player develops a game plan based on their opponent's weaknesses and strengths. They might decide to target the opponent's backhand, mix up the pace of shots, or adjust their positioning to gain an advantage.

  Traders also develop strategies based on their analysis of the market. They might use technical analysis, fundamental analysis, or a combination of both to identify patterns, trends, and support/resistance levels to enter or exit a trade. Like tennis, trading often involves anticipating the behavior of others (like the market or other traders) and adjusting one's tactics accordingly.

- **Patience and timing**

  Tennis players must exercise patience and wait for the right opportunity to strike. A tennis player may rally with their opponent, waiting for a weak return, and then go for a winner when the opportunity arises.

  In trading, timing is everything. Sometimes the best action is doing nothing and waiting for a clear, high-probability setup to develop. A trader may need to patiently wait for the right entry point or the right market conditions to align before taking action, just like a tennis player waiting for an opportunity to attack.

- **Managing emotions**

  A tennis player often faces intense emotions during a match, stress, frustration, exhilaration, and disappointment. Staying mentally strong, controlling emotions, and focusing on the next point is crucial for success.

  Traders also face emotional challenges. The market's ups and downs can trigger feelings of fear, greed, or frustration. Successful traders, like successful tennis players, are aware of these emotions, learn to manage them, keeping a clear head and sticking to their strategy even in tough times.

- **Consistency and discipline**

  Top tennis players train for years to develop consistent strokes, solid footwork, and a disciplined approach to their game. Even during a match, consistency, playing each point well, matters more than any single shot.

Consistency is equally important in trading. A trader who develops and sticks to a **consistent trading plan** over time, adjusting only when necessary, based on solid data, is more likely to be successful in the long term than someone who frequently jumps between strategies.

- **Dealing with losses**

  In tennis, even the best players lose matches or points. What matters is how they react to losses. Successful players use losses as learning experiences and focus on improving their game, rather than dwelling on past mistakes.

  Losses are an unavoidable part of any performance-driven discipline. What defines long-term success is not their absence, but the response to them. Maintaining confidence, respecting risk parameters, and extracting lessons from unfavorable outcomes allows progress without emotional disruption or deviation from a well-defined strategy.

- **The importance of practice**

  Success in tennis comes from consistent practice. The more a player practices their technique, footwork, and mental approach, the better they perform in matches.

  In the same way, trading skill develops through deliberate practice. Backtesting strategies, reviewing past trades, journaling decisions, managing risk, refining execution, recognizing unproductive or "bad" days, respecting limits, and training emotional discipline all contribute to the consistency required for long-term profitability.

- **Game-time focus vs. pre-game preparation**

  Much like the pre-match preparation (physical conditioning, mental readiness), tennis players spend a lot of time practicing and preparing for the match itself. When the match begins, all the preparation comes into play, and the player needs to stay focused on executing the plan.

  A trader spends time preparing and visualizing (researching the market, analysing charts, developing a trading plan), and when the market opens, it's all about execution. The pre-trade and pre-market analysis is crucial. The ability to execute the plan in real-time and adjust when necessary is what leads to success.

- **Learning from experience**

  Every match, win or lose, teaches something valuable. A tennis player learns from their opponent's strengths and weaknesses, adjusts their strategies, and refines their skills.

  Every trade, whether profitable or not, offers a lesson. Traders learn from their wins and losses, analyzing what went well or what went wrong to improve their future decisions.

17 MANIPULATION TECHNIQUES

17.1 WHY IS IT IMPORTANT TO KNOW THEM?

Stock market manipulation refers to possible actions taken by individuals or entities to artificially influence the price of a financial instrument (like a stock or a future contract) to their own benefit.

Understanding the main manipulation tactics allows you to reduce the chance of being influenced by these techniques, better assess potential risks in the market, and stay focus.

Most of the time it is about avoiding buying or selling at manipulated prices and focusing on your own analysis instead of reacting to artificial price movements.

Most market manipulation techniques are illegal in many countries, but in trading some of them are part of the business and widely used.

> ***MARKET MANIPULATION IS THE ARTIFICIAL INFLUENCE OF THE PRICE OF A FINANCIAL INSTRUMENT TO BENEFIT FROM IT***

17.2 HERD BEHAVIOR

Big institutions and analysts can encourage retail traders to act in unisono, by emphasizing particular stock picks or news, which might lead to a predictable buying or selling behavior.

Professionals know this emotional herd behavior and use it in their favor, buying when retail traders are fearful and selling when they are euphoric. They know that this overreaction is temporary, so they may wait for the market to overreact and then capitalize on the inevitable correction once retail traders have moved in and out.

This phenomenon is the so-called **contrarian** approach.

17.3 RETAIL TRADERS ARE PREDICTABLE

Many retail traders use popular, widely available tools (e.g., MACD, RSI, fibonacci levels and other indicators) and follow simplified strategies, commonly taught in free or mass-market trading courses, often distributed through media or mainstream educational content.

This widely consumed knowledge leads to a similar and predictable behavior:

- Retail traders place their entries or stop-loss orders just below or above commonly expected levels or candlestick patterns generating large buy and sell volumes.
- They also respond similarly to specific patterns or setups - e.g. reacting to a breakout at a particular resistance level or entering long at a green pin bar regardless of its position on the chart.

Professional traders and institutions know this predictable behavior and use it to their advantage.

17.4 RETAIL TRADERS AS LIQUIDITY SOURCE

By anticipating where retail traders will place their entries, stop-losses and target prices, professional traders know where to find the liquidity they need to trade big volumes in the market.

As I said in Chapter 2.3 retail traders provide consistent liquidity to professional traders and to bigger institutions, making it easier for professional traders to execute large orders without causing significant price disruptions or slippage.

The activity of retails traders can also be even tracked, using algorithms and advanced tools, where it is possible to see where stops and entry orders are stacked.

> ***PROFESSIONAL TRADERS CAN PROGRAM THEIR SYSTEMS TO ENTER OR EXIT POSITIONS WHEN THEY ANTICIPATE THAT A LARGE NUMBER OF RETAIL TRADERS ARE LIKELY TO ACT IN A CERTAIN WAY***

17.5 MOVING THE MARKET

As retail traders often place their orders at predictable levels, professional traders can also use this knowledge to manipulate, influence and move the market by triggering these orders.

Big institutions can place trades with large volumes which can move the price in a certain direction. These manipulated market movements, even the smaller ones, can be used to trigger the orders of retail traders in two ways:

- To hunt stop-losses.
- To create false breakouts.

17.6 STOP-LOSS HUNTING

When stop-loss orders are triggered, a sharp price movement can be generated, forcing retail traders to exit their positions at a loss. This phenomenon is called "stop-loss hunting". Professional traders can take advantage of the liquidity delivered by these price movements or participate in the movement itself.

Stop-loss hunting, while controversial, is generally permitted in most financial markets and is considered a legal trading practice when conducted within market regulations.

17.7 FALSE BREAKOUTS

Another way of profiting from the liquidity given by retail traders is by moving the market in a way that their entry orders are triggered and then pushing price in the opposite direction.

The most common way is creating failing breakouts, also called traps, see Chapter 6.4.4.

Professionals know that retail traders love to trade breakouts and these levels are a cluster of entry orders. These breakout levels are a good spot to trade large volumes in the opposite direction of retail traders, without moving the market unfavorably, as they find the needed liquidity.

Using this method is possible to accumulate or distribute large positions while retail traders get shaken out.

That is the reason why most retail traders get stopped out most of the time, which could look like conspiracy, but it is not. It is just big institutions and trading firms looking for liquidity.

17.8 HOW CAN YOU AVOID THIS TECHNIQUES

- Don't cluster stops where everyone else does.
- Understand how liquidity works. Think like an institutional trader, what would you do if you had to fill a large order?
- Shift focus to context, price action, volume and order flow. They provide better insight than lagging indicators.
- Don't trade breakouts.

> ***BY ANTICIPATING HOW RETAIL TRADERS WILL REACT TO CERTAIN MARKET CONDITIONS AND SETUPS, PROFESSIONALS CAN USE THIS EXPECTED BEHAVIOR TO EXECUTE PROFITABLE TRADES***

17.9 MANIPULATION METHODS

There are many manipulation methods that have been used in the past. Here are some of them:

17.9.1 PRICE MANIPULATION

17.9.1.1 The most common price manipulation technique: spoofing

Spoofing is a disruptive algorithmic trading practice that is based on placing huge bids to buy (buy limit orders) or offers to sell (sell limit orders) financial instruments or stocks and then cancelling them before the deal is executed. The intention of these fake orders is to create a false impression of demand or supply at certain price levels and manipulate the price and the sentiment of the market.

Spoofing has become increasingly prevalent with the rise of high-frequency trading (HFT). HFT enables the execution of large trade orders within extremely short periods of time, providing opportunities for spoofers to move prices of securities to a greater extent and earn higher profits. Watching at the order book, see Chapter 19.2, you can see how this spoofing method works.

BID	Price $	ASK
	11,5	700
	11,0	900
	10,5	**20.000**
	10,0	
1.000	9,5	
900	9,0	
400	8,5	
200	8,0	

Big Sell limit order appearing and disappearing on the order book

This is a typical example of spoofing (see image above). When a large sell limit order appears, it can create the impression that a major institution intends to sell at that level, making it seem difficult for price to move higher in the short term. This often generates bearish sentiment, as a significant volume, such as 20,000 shares, would need to be absorbed for price to break above a level like 10.50.

High-frequency algorithms may place such orders to influence other market participants by creating the illusion of selling pressure. Once traders begin to react, often by selling, the large sell order is quickly removed. The resulting liquidity provided by sellers can then be used by institutions or algorithms to enter long positions with minimal slippage.

By anticipating and exploiting predictable market reactions, manipulators can profit from this behavior. Spoofing is therefore considered a form of market manipulation.

17.9.1.2 Other price manipulation techniques

Wash trading or painting the tape

Wash trading is a practice where traders are buying and selling shares at the same price, to artificially inflate the trading volume and drive the stock price up.

Front running

When a trader buys shares for their own account ahead of executing a large order for a client, causing the price to rise.

Bear raiding

Bear raiding is the coordinated selling of a stock with the goal of driving down the price.

Momentum ignition

Buying a stock in large amounts to create momentum and cause other investors to follow suit and drive up the price.

Hidden orders

Placing orders for stocks that are not visible to the public, making it difficult to determine the true supply and demand.

Laddering

When a group of investors agrees to trade a stock at increasing prices to create the impression of strong demand and drive up the price.

Fictitious trades

The creation of fake trades to manipulate the price of a stock.

Pre-arranged trading

Buying and selling a stock with pre-arranged buyers or sellers to manipulate the price.

Cornering the market

An individual or group of individuals buys up enough shares of a stock to control the market and then manipulates the price to their advantage.

Parking

Temporarily transferring ownership of shares to another party to conceal the true ownership and manipulate the stock price.

17.9.2 Manipulation of information

Some other manipulation techniques are based on the manipulation of information and news. Here are some examples:

Rumor mongering

Spreading false or misleading information about a company or stock to manipulate the price.

Window dressing

Selling poorly performing stocks and replacing them with winners just before the end of a reporting period to make the fund look better.

Boiler room operations

High-pressure sales tactics to sell worthless or overpriced stocks to unsuspecting investors.

Market manipulation through social media

Spreading false or misleading information about a stock or company through social media platforms.

Stock manipulation through news releases

Release of false or misleading news to influence the stock price.

Pump and Dump schemes

A group of investors artificially inflates the price of a stock by spreading false or misleading information, and then sell off their shares at a profit, leaving other investors with worthless stocks.

Insider trading

Using confidential or non-public information that is not available to the general public to make trades or pass it to others.

Short and distort / Bear raid

Short selling a stock and then spreading false or misleading information about the company to drive down the price and profit from the short position.

Misuse of public funds

Using public funds to artificially prop up a stock or company.

The pump and dump via email or newsletters

Sending mass emails or newsletters to promote a stock, driving up the price, then selling off shares before the price collapses.

False rumors

Spreading rumors or false information about a company to manipulate the price of its stock.

False filings

Submitting false or misleading documents to regulatory agencies to manipulate the stock price.

Pumping up earnings

A company artificially inflates its earnings by engaging in questionable accounting practices.

Round-tripping

Artificially inflating a company's revenue by selling goods or services to a shell company, then buying them back.

Ponzi schemes

An individual or group of individuals uses the money from new investors to pay off earlier investors, while giving the impression that the investment is profitable.

Delayed disclosure of news

A company delays the release of bad news to manipulate the stock price.

Mergers and acquisitions

A company makes a public announcement about a merger or acquisition to manipulate the stock price.

Improper accounting

Manipulating financial statements to misrepresent a company's financial health and inflate the stock price.

> ***THE PREVIOUS EXAMPLES DESCRIBE KNOWN MARKET MANIPULATION TECHNIQUES; HOWEVER, THIS DOES NOT IMPLY THAT THEY ARE USED BY ALL COMPANIES OR MARKET PARTICIPANTS***

17.10 MANIPULATION AND TRADING PATTERNS

Overreaction to news or earnings reports

Retail traders often react to news or earnings reports in an exaggerated way due to educational emphasis on certain news or events. Professional traders know that this overreaction is temporary, so they may wait for the market to overreact and then capitalize on the inevitable correction once the retail traders have moved in and out.

Forcing squeezes of short sellers

When short sellers are forced to buy back shares (to limit their losses) they have borrowed to cover their positions, the price can skyrocket.

It becomes problematic for short sellers when there are not enough shares outstanding to close out their positions. The share price may continue to rise unabated until the company issues new shares or shareholders agree to sell their shares. This is the only way for the short sellers to close their positions, which is why they have an unlimited risk of loss.

This results in excess demand, which can drive the price even higher and thus further increase the losses of the short sellers.

During the GameStop short squeeze in January 2021, several large institutions were heavily short the stock, expecting the price to fall. Instead, a large and coordinated group of retail traders began aggressively buying shares and call options, pushing the price sharply higher. As the stock kept rising, institutional short sellers were forced to close their positions at a huge loss, which drove the price even higher and amplified the move.

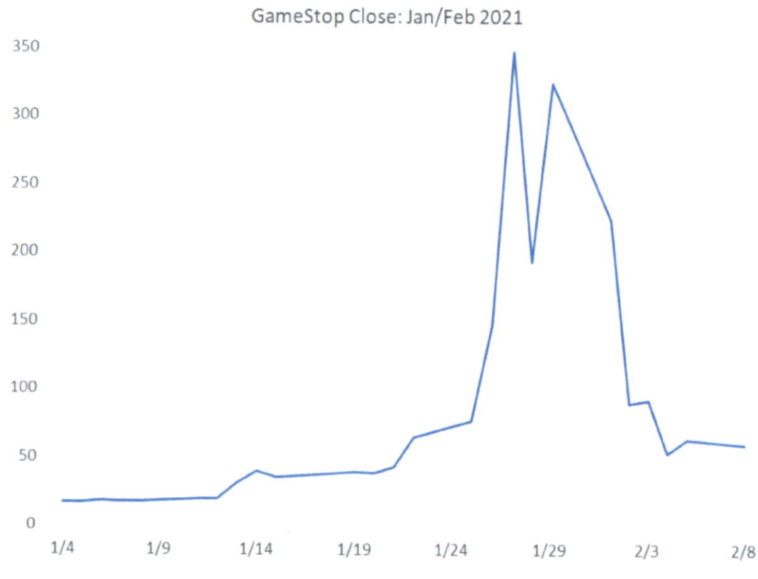

Gamestop Stock, January 2021

18 NEWS

Many news events can significantly impact the price movement of a financial asset. These events act as external catalysts, influencing prices in the short term. If you are a short-term trader, you need to understand how to deal with news events managing risk effectively.

The truth is, in the short term, it is impossible to know how price is going to react when major news is released.

Markets can become very volatile or even choppy and unpredictable after them.

Sometimes smart money seduces inexperienced and impulsive traders to go in the wrong direction, before they quickly move the market against them.

AVOID IMPULSIVE TRADING

Depending on the news, a spike in volatility is to be expected, which can trigger your stop-loss unexpectedly if you are in a trade. My personal recommendation is

DON'T TRADE BEFORE, DURING OR DIRECTLY AFTER A NEWS RELEASE

Before you start your trading session, be aware of which news is going to be released during the day and at what time, and avoid being in the market in those moments.

A good source to check news is ***www.econoday.com***

Check on them, set an alarm 5 min before, and avoid trading before, during and after the news event.

18.1 HOW CAN YOU USE NEWS?

Some events and news can generate a strong push in one direction, which can be considered the beginning of a trend. I recommend starting to look for a trade only after that moment. One possible strategy, that can be used, is the one explained in Chapter 7.8.4.1.

I know that many traders jump into movements generated by news, but there is no clear edge by doing that, as volatility can be very high.

JUST OBSERVE IF A NEW TREND STARTS AND LOOK FOR A RELIABLE PATTERN TO TRADE

18.2 OPINIONS, RECOMMENDATIONS AND ANALYST´S REPORTS

18.2.1 ANALYST'S RECOMMENDATIONS AND MARKET SENTIMENT

Investor sentiment plays a crucial role, as public opinion can drive demand for certain stocks. Positive news, social media trends, or influential figures endorsing a stock can push prices up, while negative sentiment can trigger sell-offs.

Analysts upgrades or downgrades, along with changes in price targets, can impact investor perception and potentially lead to stock price movements.

A strong "buy" recommendation from a respected analyst can attract investors, increasing demand and boosting the stock price, whereas a downgrade may lead to declines.

Be aware that social media, online forums, and even mainstream financial news outlets can be used to amplify misleading narratives.

Algorithmic trading systems, which react instantly to news, can further magnify these effects, creating rapid fluctuations.

18.3 NEWS AND THE IMPACT ON ASSET PRICES

From a short-term trader´s point of view, the following types of news have the most impact on the stock and futures market.

18.3.1 Macroeconomic data

- Economic data

Key economic indicators such as GDP growth, inflation rates, employment data, and consumer sentiment can affect the overall stock market.

- Interest rate changes

Central banks' decisions to raise or lower interest rates can impact borrowing costs, corporate profitability, and investor sentiment.

- Currency fluctuations

Exchange rate movements can affect companies that conduct business internationally, particularly those with significant foreign exposure, impacting their earnings and stock prices.

- Federal reserve announcements

Statements and decisions made by the Federal Reserve, including changes in monetary policy, can affect investor sentiment and stock market movements.

- Monetary policy decisions

Policy actions by central banks, such as quantitative easing or tightening, can have a significant impact on liquidity in the financial markets and influence stock prices.

- Global economic events

Economic events and developments in major economies, such as policy decisions by central banks, trade agreements, or geopolitical tensions, can impact global markets and stock prices.

18.3.2 Data related to a specific company or market

- Earnings reports

Strong or weak earnings results from a company or from other companies in the same sector can significantly impact a company's stock price and potentially influence the broader market sentiment.

- Company guidance

When companies provide guidance or outlook for future earnings, it can affect investor sentiment and influence stock prices.

- Total addressable market (TAM) and market outlooks

A large TAM indicates significant revenue opportunities, attracting investors and justifying higher valuations. Positive market outlooks signal industry expansion, boosting investor confidence and stock demand. Conversely, a small or shrinking market can limit growth prospects, leading to lower valuations. Analysts use TAM to estimate future earnings, and companies in high-growth industries, like AI or renewable energy, often see stronger stock performance. Overall, TAM and market forecasts shape investor expectations, influencing stock price movements in the short and long term.

- Corporate scandals.

High-profile corporate scandals or instances of fraud can lead to significant declines in stock prices, particularly for the companies involved or related entities.

- Merger and acquisition activities

Announcements of mergers, acquisitions, or divestitures can create volatility in the stock market as investors assess the potential impact on companies involved.

- Corporate actions

Stock buybacks, dividend announcements, and changes in capital structure, such as debt issuances or stock splits, can impact stock prices.

18.3.3 Sector related news

- Technological disruptions and technological advancements

Emergence of disruptive technologies, market trends, or changes in consumer behavior can impact specific industries and companies, leading to stock price fluctuations.

Breakthroughs in technology, such as advancements in artificial intelligence, renewable energy, or biotechnology, can drive stock market movements as investors evaluate the potential market impact.

- Sector-specific events:

Sector-specific catalysts, such as FDA approvals for pharmaceutical companies, breakthroughs in research and development, or changes in regulations for specific industries, can impact stock prices within those sectors.

- Regulatory changes

New regulations or changes in existing regulations can affect specific sectors or industries, potentially influencing stock prices within those areas.

18.3.4 One time Events

- Geopolitical events

Major political or geopolitical developments, such as trade wars, elections, or international conflicts, can introduce uncertainty and impact stock markets globally.

- Natural disasters or accidents

Major natural disasters, such as hurricanes, earthquakes, or pandemics, can disrupt supply chains, impact business operations, and affect stock markets globally.

19 ADVANCED TOOLS AND TECHNIQUES

There are several advanced tools and techniques, such as:

- order flow
- order book
- and times and sales (the tape)

that can help validate the strategies discussed in this book. I want to provide you with a brief overview of them, giving you a foundation, which will allow you to explore them further, should you choose to do so.

Advanced tools are often labeled as such because of their complexity, but this does not necessarily mean they are better or more effective.

Pric action alone is sufficient for making trading decisions; however, these advanced tools can provide an additional layer of confirmation and provide, in certain situations, deeper insight into market behavior.

To access these tools, you typically need to upgrade your market data subscription to Level II, which offers more detailed information about market activity.

The underlying principle behind order flow charts, the order book, and the tape is auction theory.

The stock market itself can be thought of as an **ongoing auction** in which sellers and buyers place asks (offers to sell) and bids (offers to buy). When a buyer's bid matches a seller's ask, a trade takes place.

19.1.1 HOW DOES THE AUCTION THEORY IN THE STOCK MARKET WORK?

Consider the market to be a system of two auctions:

- Bids are made by buyers (e.g., "I'll buy 100 shares at $49").
- Asks are submitted by sellers, such as "I'll sell 100 shares at $51."

A transaction takes place when the seller's ask (for example, $50) and the buyer's bid are equal.

The market price of the stock is continuously updated by this continuous process, which balances supply and demand.

> ***TOOLS LIKE ORDER FLOW CHARTS, THE ORDER BOOK AND THE TAPE (TIMES & SALES) TRY TO VISUALIZE THE DATA OF THIS CONTINUOUS AUCTION PROCESS IN A WAY THAT IS VISIBLE AND UNDERSTANDABLE TO TRADERS***

19.2 ORDER FLOW

The term "order flow" describes the market's real-time buying and selling activity, which illustrates the dynamics of supply and demand for a financial instrument.

Unlike standard candles, which only show open, high, low and the close price, order flow candles reveal the internal dynamic of who was aggressively buying and selling, and at what price levels.

> ***ORDER FLOW ANALYSIS ALLOWS TRADERS TO LOOK INSIDE CANDLES AND UNDERSTAND THE REAL-TIME DYNAMICS OF BUYING AND SELLING PRESSURE***

In Order flow charts, candles are composed of the following elements:

- Rows, which represent a specific price level within the candle's range.
- Two Columns:
    - Left column: the Bid column shows trades initiated by aggressive sellers.
    - Right column: the Ask column shows trades initiated by aggressive buyers.

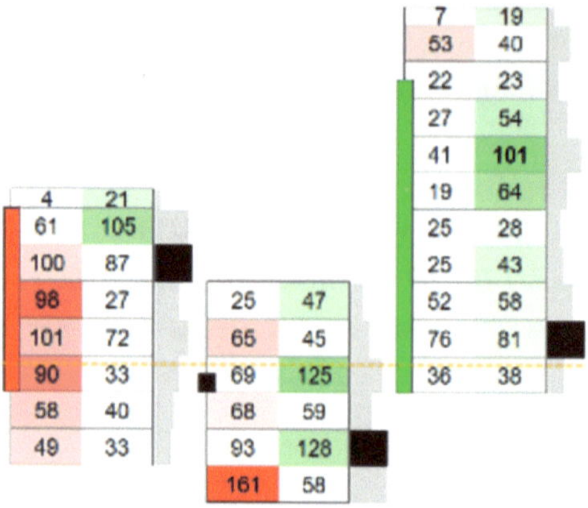

Representation of 3 candles in Order Flow

Let us analyze the second candle of the image above. At the lowest part you see a huge selling pressure (161 contracts have been aggressively sold at the bottom of the candle). After that, buyers came in, assuming that a support level hast been achieved, and were willing to buy at higher levels (see Ask column). In this case 128, 59, 125, 45 and 47 contracts has been traded/bought at the ask side, signalling a potential reversal in price.

Order flow charts allow you to analyze the microstructure of the market, as you have information about what is happening at every single price level.

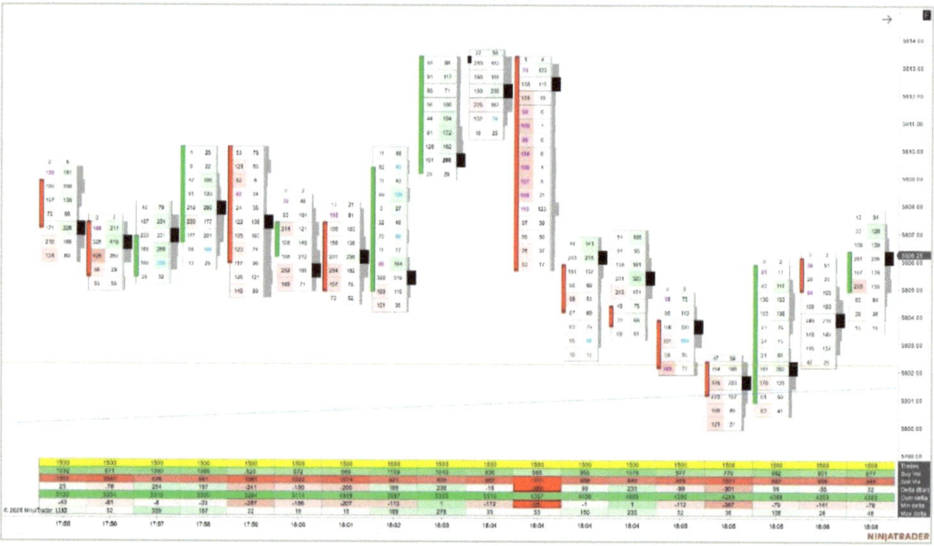

Example of order book chart. The red figures inside the big red candle signal selling pressure.

> ***If a large volume cluster appears near the bottom of a candle, it may indicate strong support***

By examining order flow, you can learn about market strength, liquidity, and possible price moves, you can better identify hidden buying or selling pressure and you can define your entries, exits, and stop placements with greater precision.

For instance, persistently aggressive bid-side buying could be a hint of high demand and a possible price increase.

Example of an order flow chart. Green figures show buying pressure, while red figures indicate selling pressure. Price moves up and down accordingly in this case.

19.2.1 Imbalances

With order flow, you can also easily identify imbalances in the market. Imbalances are situations where there is a significant difference between buy and sell orders at specific price levels. If buy orders at a certain price level are consistently larger than sell orders, it suggests strong demand and potential upward price movement.

Example of imbalances inside a red candle, as indicator of selling pressure.

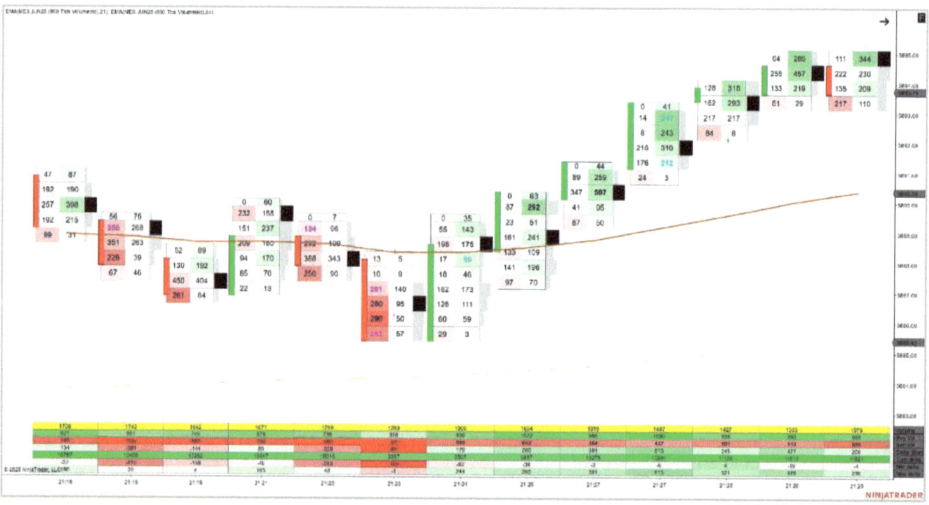

Example of a big volume cluster at swing low (where 201, 280, 290, 243 contracts have been sold without moving the price further down), indicating a potential support level.

19.3 ORDER BOOK

The order book provides a real-time snapshot of all active buy and sell limit orders for a given asset, showing liquidity and market depth.

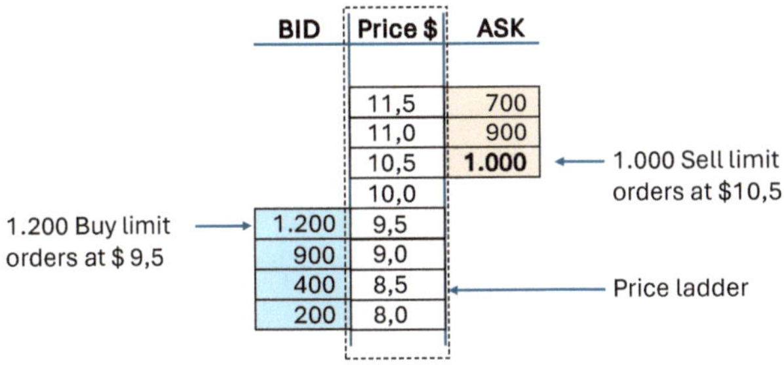

Example of a price ladder with buy limit orders on the bid side and sell limit orders on the ask side.

With the order book you will be able to spot hidden liquidity, spoofing activities, and identifying support and resistance levels.

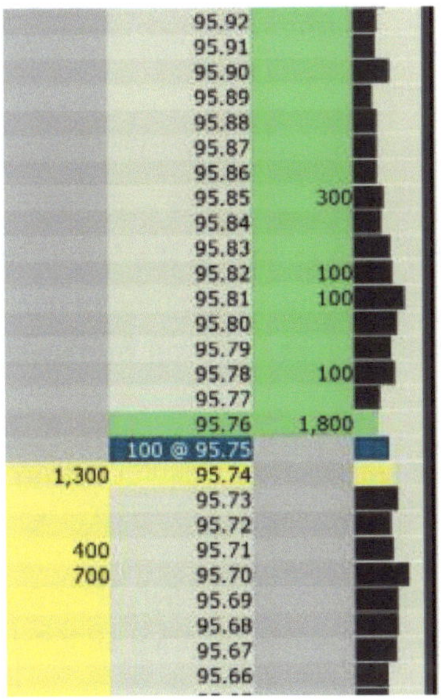

Order book. BABA stock. On the left column you see 1.300 buy limit orders at $95,74. On the right column you find 1.800 sell limit orders at $95,76. And in the middle you see the price ladder with the filled-executed orders, see a transaction of 100 stocks at $95,75.

IT HELPS TRADERS UNDERSTAND SUPPLY AND DEMAND AT VARIOUS PRICE LEVELS

If there is a large buy wall (significant bid orders) at a certain price, it may act as a support level, preventing price from falling further. Conversely, a large sell wall can serve as a resistance level.

Institutional traders use the order book to improve trade execution by entering orders where liquidity is highest, reducing slippage. Additionally, order book imbalances, where buy orders far exceed sell orders or vice versa, can hint at potential price movements, allowing traders to position themselves accordingly.

A larger bid side might suggest strong buying interest or a potential upward move. Whereas a larger ask side might signal selling pressure or resistance.

WHILE ADVANCED TOOLS OFFER AN ADDITIONAL LAYER OF CONFIRMATION FOR TRADING DECISIONS, THEY ALSO INTRODUCE MORE COMPLEXITY

19.4 TIMES AND SALES

The Time and Sales window, also known as the "tape," shows real-time traded data, including price, volume, and execution time of each transaction. It is quite common to use Time and Sales in conjunction with order flow analysis to validate trade entries and exits.

With this tool you can get a feeling of the market activity, identifying where large institutional orders are being executed.

A series of rapid, high-volume trades at the ask price may indicate strong buying pressure, while a similar pattern at the bid price suggests selling pressure.

IF YOU SEE REPEATED LARGE BUYS IN THE TIMES AND SALES WINDOW ALONG WITH STRONG BID SUPPORT IN THE ORDER BOOK, IT MAY CONFIRM A BULLISH TRADE SETUP.

Reading the tape correctly takes time. Be patient, practice, and observe it as much as you can.

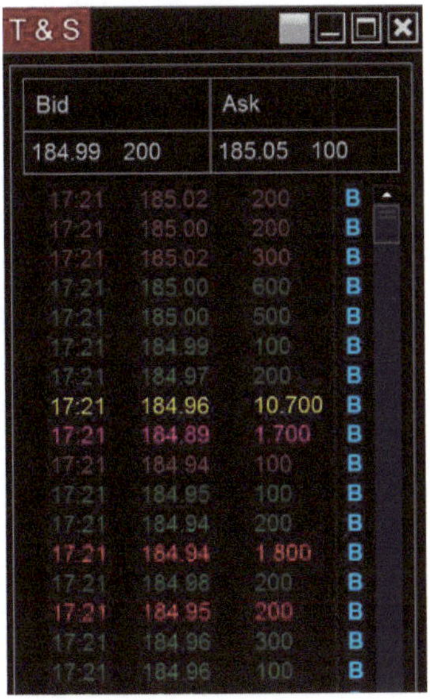

Example of a Time & Sales window.

> ***A SERIES OF RAPID, HIGH-VOLUME TRADES ARE A SIGN OF MOMENTUM IN THE MARKET***

Example of a Time & Sales, order book and volume profile. ES futures contract. 1500 tich chart.

The combination of Order Flow, Time and Sales, and Order Book analysis provides you with valuable information about the market mechanics, allowing you to refine entry points with greater precision.

Professional traders monitor imbalances to anticipate where price may go next, especially when combined with order flow, tape reading, and volume delta.

For example, if there is a buy-side imbalance and you see aggressive buying in the footprint chart (ask volume increasing), that can strengthen the bullish signal.

20 RECOMMENDATIONS

I want to share with you a list I have developed over more than 10 years, with ideas, tips, and recommendations for your trading practice.

Go through this list regularly and make it grow according to your needs. Some of these points may sound trivial or simple, but they are truly the key:

- Buy low, sell high.
- Do not predict.
- Wait for candles to close. Sometimes a red pin bar becomes a green candle or the other way around. Only finished candles matter!
- Observe in which zones traps and mini traps are happening: some big players might be looking for liquidity.
- Traps are better than breakouts.
- 1 min chart is too volatile. If you trade stocks, go for 2 min or 5 min charts at least.
- If you trade futures, use tick charts. You will find more patterns.
- Strong moves often end in Climax patterns with high volume and RSI under 10.
- Don't enter a falling knife; you never know when it ends.
- The market opening can be very choppy; be disciplined and wait for a clear market structure.
- Wait for the first target price to be reached before you move your stop-loss.
- Observe what happens when stop-loss positions of opponent traders are triggered.
- Only hold a position overnight if you have enough liquidity and if momentum is very strong in different time frames.
- Failures usually generate good runs.

- If a very good-looking signal fails, exit the trade right away.
- Even if there is very positive news about a company, a stock can move downward.
- A market can stay crazy and wrong longer than you can hold your position.
- A trend can last longer than you could imagine. Don't predict the end of the trend. Just trade what you see.
- I doesn't matter if you are right. The market will decide independently.
- If there is no recognizable market structure, don't trade.
- 1st retest of major trendlines are good spots to look for entry signals.
- Many retail traders lose their accounts in a few days, thinking that they cannot be wrong all the time.
- Trade only if you have enough time and patience to recover. It is like a tennis match. If you play to win, you would only play it if you had enough time to finish the match.
- Decrease your risk at the end of a trading session.
- Never predict or expect something to happen. Observe and decide on what you see, and not on what you think.
- Compare trades and signals and prioritize. Analyze if they have or would have achieved the 1st target price.
- If you see contradictory market structures and signals, wait for more confirmation and information.
- The market is limitless. Don't rush.
- The market will still be here tomorrow, ready to offer new opportunities, if you need to wait, it's worth the patience.
- Be very rigorous and demanding. Set high standards for your trades.
- Learn to miss trades; it is better than to lose them.
- Volume validates price, but remember, it can be faked.

- If you trade with high leverage, be aware of the increased risk and always use a stop-loss.
- If a resistance or support level is not retested, there may be urgency in the market. A strong trend could be forming.
- A prolonged trend upward can end abruptly.
- In a prolonged trend downward, sellers will try to move the price lower several times.
- Be aware of price magnets in the market.
- Prolonged trends: look for traps in different timeframes.
- The failure of good-looking trades is an even better trade.
- Pin bar candles at trap levels, plus huge confluence, are the best entry signals.
- Try to understand why price moves the way it moves.
- If you trade stock options, be cautious about trading them on Friday before expiration. This is one of the riskiest financial products to trade on that day.
- Candlestick patterns work best at higher timeframes.
- In lower timeframes, look for patterns and entry signals.
- Don't overtrade; 5 trades a day is more than enough.
- Before you enter a trade, visualize what you want to see and wait for that moment.
- It is normal to feel fear on certain days. Accept it and wait for a better day. Sometimes, it's not the market at all, but your own state of mind.
- Enough profit potential in 2 different timeframes is a good context for a trade.
- Avoid trades if there is a clear trendline on the way up or down. Make sure there is enough space for the price to move.
- Train in playback mode.

- Train with small position sizes and real money.
- Increase size gradually, even if your results are excellent.
- Don't look at the money (your PnL) you are making. Look at the RR risk-reward rate of your trades.

Author

Carlos Bermejo Pascual studied industrial engineering and electronics in Valencia (Spain) and developed an early interest in the stock market. An interest strongly influenced by his mother, who successfully managed her own private fund.

He moved to Germany in 1998. His fascination with investing and trading, combined with a strong drive to analyze and refine strategies, led him to adopt a scientific and systematic approach to the markets. Over more than a decade, he dedicated himself to studying price charts, coding algorithms, and developing and implementing effective trading strategies for liquid financial instruments.

Coaching

Carlos offers **personalized coaching programs** in English, Spanish, and German for traders seeking structured guidance, discipline, and accountability.

Due to limited availability, coaching is offered on an **application basis only**. If you are looking for a dedicated accountability partner and tailored support, you are invited to submit a request for consideration.

Feedback

If you have any questions or would like to share feedback about this book, your message is always welcome.
Please feel free to get in touch by email.

Thanks for your interest and enjoy the journey of trading!

Email

trading@trading.si-investing.com

www.trading.si-investing.com

www.ingramcontent.com/pod-product-compliance
Lightning Source LLC
Chambersburg PA
CBHW041308210926
51850CB00011B/2928
* 9 7 8 3 0 0 0 8 5 8 2 1 5 *